Raised REDNECK

CHARLES LEMAR BROWN

Broken L Press

To Doug Gray, Dennis Russell,
Dennis Brown, & Rollan Dennis

Contents

DEAR READERS,

Who gets to decide which side is the wrong side? Is it those with money? Those with power? I don't have the answers, but I do know that as far as I'm concerned, I was born on the right side. Most towns have a line of separation. For many that is a set of railroad tracks. Songs and stories have been written about people from the wrong side of the tracks. It's not a new concept, hell even Shakespeare used it in one of his most famous plays.

The town I grew up in wasn't divided by tracks. It was divided by a creek. On one side of this magical waterway were the people with power and money. There are those who would say these folks lived on the right side of the tracks. I would strongly disagree. Why, you might ask. Well, it's simple, that's not where I was raised, so how could it be the right side? I was born and grew up on the other side, the countryside, the backwoods side, the redneck side.

On my side of the creek, we stood for God and country and family. We all went to church in a little white building right on the banks of the creek and afterwards we had our Sunday afternoon meal at Ma Essary's house. The same house where every evening Poppa Ebb sat on the front porch reading the Good Book to his ole red hound dog while sipping on his very own homemade shine.

It's where I learned to walk and talk. Where I caught my first fish, killed my first deer, and wrecked my first truck. Where I tasted my first kiss and received my first broken heart. Where I made my first trip to the alter to ask the Lord to forgive me for smashing Jimbo's lip. And where Jimbo made his first trip to the alter to ask God to forgive him for blacking my eye.

If you're still not convinced it was the right side, then let me leave you to think on this. It's the place I was born. The place the Good Lord chose for me to be brought into this world and the place He planned for me to be raised. So, for me the answer is very simple, the reason my side of the creek was the right side is because it was the side God chose for me. And therefore, the reason I was raised redneck.

ELECTRICITY 101

Peeing on an electric fence is a fine art. One that takes a great deal of patience and practice. By the time we reached our teenage years, both Jimbo and I had become experts. Now you may be thinking, what's the big deal? You just walk up to a strand of electrified fence, whip out the ole tallywacker, and let'er rip. And that my friend is where you would be wrong. Not only wrong, but in a great deal of pain.

You see, electricity is a funny thing—it likes to travel. And when it gets started, it moves like greased lightning. Now, the neat thing about peeing on an electric fence is the way it spits and sputters when the urine comes in contact with the metal. However, it ain't nearly as funny if that electrical current makes it way upstream to the headwater, so it's mighty important to control the flow.

There are a multitude of tried and true methods that will keep you from electrifying your manhood, but I prefer the pinch and release method. This allows for short burst of liquid to strike the fence, but not a solid stream, so the electricity can't find its way back to the source. Jimbo would argue that the figure eight technique he uses is the best, but he'd be wrong. He won't admit it, but I've seen him grimace on more than one occasion.

I recall the summer that I turned fourteen. That's the summer Aunt Beatrice and Uncle Harv came to visit and brought along their daughter, Jessica. Jimbo immediately fell in love with her and the more I tried to explain it just wasn't right, them being second cousins and all, the more he refused to listen. She was a year older than me and nearly three years older than Jimbo but he said age didn't count for much. The bigger problem was that she had a boyfriend who had just turned sixteen and could drive. None of this deterred Jimbo—no sir, not for a split second. His mind was made up.

Jessica's boyfriend, Randy, seemed like a nice enough fella to me, but Jimbo was my first cousin and closer on the family tree, so naturally I had to side with him. Now once Jimbo gets an idea in his pea-brain, there just ain't no knocking it out, and he was dead set on running Randy off.

Some years back Uncle Harv had been selling them fancy Hoover vacuums door to door and that's how he met up with Aunt Beatrice. Ma Essary says Beatrice took one look at him in his fancy suit and decided she wanted him. She said once the woman got her hook into him and set, there weren't no way Harv was getting loose. Poppa Ebb had a different take on the whole situation, he said it wasn't the hook that got old Harv in trouble, it was the bait, then he laughed so hard he durn near choked on his snuff.

Whatever it was that Aunt Beatrice used, Uncle Harv married her and took her up to the big city to live in one of those fancy houses like what you see on those soaps Ma's always watching in the afternoon after the sweepin' and moppin's done. I overheard Auntie Mae, Jimbo's momma, telling the neighbor lady that it had been eight years since she laid eyes on them. She said there weren't no way she was gonna stoop and bow just because they thought they was better'n her 'cause they lived up in the city. I kinda got the feelin' Auntie Mae wished she'd seen ole Harv first, but I could be wrong on that one.

After two days of watching Jessica and Randy jetting here, there, and yonder in his little blue roadster, Jimbo'd had about all he could take. After dinner, the two of them started out for the car and as they stepped down off the porch, Jimbo started giggling.

"What's so funny?" Randy turned and asked.

Now Jimbo really turned it on. He rolled back on the porch and started laughing so hard I thought he was gonna bust something.

4

"Hey!!!??" Randy shouted, "What's so dang funny!!??

I stood up off the old wooden stool that I'd been sittin' on and walked over to where Jimbo was still rollin' around giggling. After a minute, he quit laughing, sat up, and wiped at his eyes.

"Harold," he said and winked at me. "I just think it's funny how Randy here thinks he's so tough," Jimbo snorted, "a really bad, city boy."

"I can whip you." Randy said through clinched teeth, red color rising from under his collar and into his face.

"Maybe," Jimbo grins, "but then you're four years older than me and nearly a foot taller, so how tough would that be?"

It occurred to me that standing on the porch as I was, I was lookin' Randy right straight in the eye. And I was beginning to doubt if we could take him even if the both of us tagged in together and set to beatin' on him. It was beginning to look like, as usual, Jimbo's big mouth was gonna get both of our butts kicked.

"So," Randy snarled.

"So," Jimbo returned. "How 'bout a test? Let's see who's tougher, city or country."

"Let's do it," Randy punctuated his words by spitting on the ground in front of Jimbo's old, scuffed boots.

"Come on," Jessica pulled at his shirt sleeve. "They're just dumb kids."

I didn't have to look down to feel Jimbo tense. Those words cut him to the core, and I'm pretty sure all that love that had been building up for Jessica left him in one fell swoop. Kinda like a blown-up balloon that's let loose, his poor ole heart just deflated and sunk to the ground right there next to Randy's spit.

"Come on then," he said to Randy, but he was glaring at Jessica.

Jimbo started out around the house with Randy in tow. Jessica stomped out to his car, leaned up against it, and started pouting. Wild hogs couldn't have kept me from followin' along to see what kind of test Jimbo had in mind.

Ma Essary's garden was back behind the house and on a piece farther than that was Poppa Ebb's orchard with two big pear trees, a couple of apple trees, several plum trees, and one great big ole pecan tree. Just past them trees, Poppa Ebb had a three-strand electric fence strung to keep the cows from getting into the orchard and garden.

Jimbo marched right through the garden. Randy followed, leaning slightly forward, hands clinched, arms stiff at his sides. At the edge of the orchard, Jimbo started whistling. I shook my head and grinned, thinking, *this is gonna be interesting*, but when we passed that peach tree, I swear I could hear Ma Essary cuttin' off switches.

Just past the pecan tree, Jimbo stopped and said, "Time to separate the men from the boys." He grinned and stretched his hand out palm up presenting the electric fence much like one of Barker's Beauties would present an expensive diamond ring on *The Price Is Right*.

"I ain't touching that." Randy snarled, "That's just stupid."

"Yeah, that would be stupid," Jimbo agreed with a nod and another sly wink at me. "Any wimp can touch an electric fence. That don't prove how tough you are."

"So, what're you getting at then?" Randy wanted to know.

"Well," Jimbo stared up at him, squinted his eyes down like the actors do in those spaghetti westerns, curled up one corner of his mouth, and whispered, "betcha ain't tough enough to pee on that fence."

"Yeah, right," Randy laughed nervously. "You first."

Had Jimbo known that Poppa Ebb had replaced the ole fence charger the week before, he might have thought twice about what occurred next. But he didn't know and I ain't real sure that even if he'd had been told that the Feed Store'd had a sale on chargers and Poppa had bought one three times more powerful than the one he replaced, that Jimbo wouldn't have gone ahead as planned.

Next thing I knew, Jimbo's got his back to us and his

tallywacker out. He threw his left hand up in the air like he was ridin' a bull and I could tell from the way his right elbow was movin' he'd gone into his figure eight technique. He started whoopin' and hollerin' and laughin' like a maniac, all the time lettin' loose. That fence was sizzlin' and sparkin' every time the urine hit it and I could tell every once in a while, when the electricity made it back to the source 'cause Jimbo's free hand clinched and his scrawlin' raised an octave or two. Finally, he ended with a good ole fashion "YeeeHawww," put his member away, and zipped his trousers.

Randy was standing there looking at him like he'd lost his mind, but he didn't walk away. "What's the trick?" he finally asked.

"No trick." Jimbo held up the Boy Scout three finger sign. Just so ya know, neither me nor Jimbo, were ever in the Boy Scouts.

Randy looked over at me and I cain't tell you exactly why I did it, but I bellied up to that electic fence, unzipped, and let'er rip. Now as I said before, I use the pinch and release method, and I've perfected it to the point that it would take a trained eye to tell there is a break in the stream. So, I've got what looks like a straight full-on stream on the middle strand. I clinched my teeth and hissed through them like the current is really getting to me. About halfway through, I started growling like a rabid dog and finished with a howl that would make the hair stand up on the back of your neck. I zipped up, turned around, and gave him my toughest glare.

"Now that's tough." Jimbo spat on the ground in front of Randy and turned to walk off.

"I'm tough enough," Randy said and stepped up to the fence.

"Yeah, right," Jimbo turned back. "You'll quit as soon as the juice hits your little city boy wee wee."

"Won't either," Randy shot back, already unzipping.

"I got five dollars says he ain't tough enough." Jimbo looked over at me. "You wanna bet, Harold?"

Before, I could say yea, nay, or maybe, Randy let loose a full stream directly on that fence. I guess he'd decided the figure eight technique would work better, because as soon as the juice hit him that left hand went straight up in the air and he stiffened up like the old cigar Indian downtown in front of the liquor store. After a couple seconds, he started kinda shimmin' all over and stood straight up on his tiptoes. The stance and the sounds coming out of him reminded me of the last time we went down to the church house and Mrs. Annabelle Biggsbee started talking in tongues. When the current finally broke, Randy grabbed himself with both hands, dropped to his knees, and then rolled up right there on the ground like a baby in a womb. I had never seen anything like it in my short life and have never seen anything like it since. He just laid there weepin' and cryin' and holdin' himself.

I gotta say, I really felt sorry for him right about then, but not nearly as sorry as I did for Jimbo when Ma Essary found out about what we'd done. Yeah, I got myself switched pretty good, but poor ole Jimbo couldn't sit for weeks.

The folks out to the hospital said Randy would be just fine and gave him some pills to take for the pain and swelling. Aunt Beatrice and Uncle Harv left that night and we never saw them again. Ma told me years later that Jessica and Randy got married after high school, but they never had any kids. I'm not sure if that was because they didn't want any or not.

I asked Jimbo once, if he ever felt bad about what we'd done. He pursed his lips, nodded his head yes, then held up the Boy Scout three finger sign and laughed.

DISCIPLINE 101

Ma Essary was the sweetest mean person you'd ever want to meet. She could make you feel like you were the most special person in the world one minute then turn right around and make you want to crawl in a hole the next instant. If she had a filter, I never saw it. She pretty much said whatever came into her mind, and I never met anyone brave enough to question her. I think that may be the reason Poppa Ebb spent so much time out on the front porch with the Good Book and his moonshine.

When I was just shy of seven, and Jimbo was five-and-a-half years old, we learned one of the most important lessons of our lives. Even today, I would rank it up in the top ten. It all started innocently enough. Momma and Aunt Mae had both worn out their Sunday-go-to-church dresses—or so they claimed. Truth be told, they'd both been dieting for the last three months, and their clothes just didn't fit anymore. Whatever the reason, and since when does a woman really need a reason to go clothes shopping, it was decided that Jimbo and me would stay with Ma Essary.

Poppa Ebb, upon finding out it would be both of us, had decided the fish must be bitin' down at the creek and had skinned out in his old truck before we got there. Looking back, I can't say as I blame him. Me, by myself, I could be a handful. Not that I was a terrible, awful kid, I was just very hyper and always on the go. Jimbo, on the other hand, was not only twice as hyper as I was, but he also had an ornery streak a mile wide.

Ma Essary met us at the door in her usual cotton dress and white apron. She smiled and waved Momma and Aunt Mae off.

"Y'all come give Ma Essary a hug." She ordered with outstretched arms and we rushed in. She smelled like cookies and

I just knew it was gonna be a great day. Ma Essary's chocolate chip cookies, to this day, have never been outdone.

The minute Aunt Mae's little red car disappeared, Ma Essary hustled us through the house and into the kitchen. A heaping plate of those famous chocolate chip cookies and two glasses of ice-cold milk were already waiting on the table. Me and Jimbo set to seein' how many cookies we could eat—we'd always been kind of competitive—and before long we had completely stuffed ourselves. Talk about three very happy people. The only thing Ma Essary liked better than cooking was watching someone enjoy her cooking, and me and Jimbo had thoroughly enjoyed them cookies.

Ma Essary shooed us into the living room, started cleaning up, and getting stuff ready for lunch.

Me and Jimbo set to fussin'.

"Hey," he said to me, "I was gonna set in Poppa Ebb's chair."

"So," I told him, "I got here first."

Now, they say I when I was born, I looked like a chimpanzee. Not because I was all hairy or anything like that, but I had this long body with long arms and legs to match. For most of my childhood, that was the physique I was blessed with. Jimbo on the other hand was built like a little bulldog—big head, big shoulders, tiny waist, and short stubby, bowed legs. I was always a head taller than Jimbo, but he always outweighed me.

When I refused to give up Poppa Ebb's chair, he grabbed me by my right foot at the ankle, placed both of his feet against the edge of the seat, and heaved. Poppa Ebb would have been so proud of him. He was a big WWF Wrestling fan and us boys never missed a chance to watch it with him. Anyway, I came out of that chair airborne, flew halfway across the room, and landed with a thud. The second I came to a stop, I spun around, took two long steps, and launched. Jimbo was just crawling up into the chair, and I caught him square in the back. He grabbed a handful of the chair cushion, and I grabbed him around the waist. Hulk Hogan would have been proud of me for the amount of height I managed on that suplex. For those of you who aren't familiar with wrestling, the suplex is a move where one wrestler picks up another wrestler, throws himself backwards, and both collide violently with the floor. The only problem here was that the living room had hardwood floors, so when mine and Jimbo's head collided with that surface, it did not give like the floor of the wrestling rings on Poppa Ebb's television set.

By the time, Ma Essary made it in from the kitchen, we were both rolling around on the floor, bawling, with our heads in our hands. When we were finally able to explain to her what had happened, she was none too happy. Because I was the oldest and supposed to be setting the example—Ma Essary's words, not mine—I got the worst of the scolding.

After checking each of our heads to make sure we weren't bleedin' and there were no bones showin' through our scalps, she set us on opposite ends of her couch, turned on the television, and returned to the kitchen. My favorite show was *The Lone Ranger* and it was on, so all-in-all, I was feeling better. Jimbo, however, was still nursing a grudge.

"I don't like this show," he growled from his end of the couch.

"Well, I do." I snapped back.

He crawled down from his assigned seat and headed for the television. "I wanna watch cartoons."

"No." I shouted and raced across the room to block him from turnin' the channel.

Arms and legs spread wide; I wasn't thinkin' about how I'd left my midsection wide open. Jimbo swung from the hip and caught me square in the stomach. I doubled up and tried to catch my breath. When I raised up, I could see in Jimbo's eyes that he wasn't done. Still gasping for air, I started flailing with both arms. I had just took in another gulp of air, when Ma Essary grabbed us up by the collars and held us apart. The look on her face said that she was most definitely not happy.

"I think it's time to go outside." She said already moving towards the back door.

She had grown up picking cotton with her family, and Poppa Ebb use to brag there wasn't anyone around who could out pick her. He said the first time he laid eyes on her, she was toting a hundred-pound bag of cotton down a row and making it look easy. Neither me nor Jimbo weighed a hundred pounds. On the trip through the house, I don't think Jimbo's feet ever hit the floor once. Because I was taller, I could feel the toes of my shoes draggin' across the kitchen tile every now and again.

Ma Essary dropped us both on the back steps with a thud and headed out across the yard. Too scared to move, we just sat and watched her go. She marched right through the garden and into Poppa Ebb's orchard. Stopping at the peach tree, she pulled out the Uncle Henry pocketknife she always kept in her apron pocket and cut a limb.

For those of you who didn't grow up redneck, when an angry parent or grandparent cuts a limb from a tree, it becomes a switch. And a switch is only used for one thing. So, me and Jimbo had a pretty good idea what was coming, and I'll be honest, the thought of making a run for it did cross my mind.

When Ma Essary cut a second limb and began to remove the leaves, I looked over at Jimbo. He looked just as confused as I was, and when I looked back, Ma Essary was strippin' the leaves for a third switch. Too scared to move, we watched with big eyes as she stomped back through that garden toward us. She stopped at the edge of the porch and handed each of us a switch.

"Get up." She ordered.

Still confused, we both stood up and stepped off the porch and into the yard. I should probably mention here that it was summertime, and both me and Jimbo were in short pants.

"You two want to fight and fuss and hit each other, huh?" she asked. This was not the same woman who had given us cookies less than an hour ago. The sweet was gone and I was scared. When neither of us responded, she continued, "Howard you're the oldest so you get to go first." She pointed her switch at me and ordered, "Switch him."

I could not believe what she was saying. I just stood there shocked.

"I said switch him." She repeated and her eyes squinted down.

"I don't want to..." I started to say when her switch descended and caught me across the back of my legs just above my knees.

The sting was instant, as was the shriek that left my throat, and I began to dance in place.

"Jimbo, switch Howard." Ma Essary ordered.

Jimbo had no reservations. He swung that switch like he was playing baseball and swinging for the fence. The switch caught me the same place Ma Essary's switch had, and I let out another shriek, higher in pitch and longer in duration.

"Howard, you switch..." Ma Essary started.

Before she could finish, I swung. My first swing made contact with the back of Jimbo's legs, and he squealed and began to dance, his chubby, little legs nothin' but a blur. For the next few minutes, it was an all-out switchin'. Ma Essary stood to one side and watched as me and Jimbo whooped on each other like we'd lost our minds. We were a dancin' and a switchin, cryin' and bawlin', and slingin, snot, and then out of nowhere, Jimbo started begging for forgiveness.

In between dancin' and squealin', he started hollerin', "Oh Lord, please forgive me, I dun messed up good. Oh Lord, please help Ma Essary come to her senses. Please, please, make this here switchin' stop."

I don't know what part of that prayer upset her, but Ma Essary stepped back in and took over. She grabbed me by the collar and set me aside then went to switchin' Jimbo good. I stood there watchin' her lay into him, and a part of me felt a little sorry for him. Then without warning, Ma Essary spun around and laid one last lash across my legs. I don't know if it was because she saw sympathy in my eyes or just so she got the last switch in on both of us, but it caught me off guard and set me to squealin' all over again.

15

"Next time y'all decide you want to fight at Ma Essary's house, y'all remember this," she said as she took our switches from us. "Y'all can just stay outside the rest of the day. Wanna act like animals, you can stay outside like animals." She added as she stormed back into the house.

When Momma and Aunt Mae got back from shopping, we were still outside. I don't know if either of them ever knew about us fightin' or the switchin', but I know I never spoke of it. I can't say me and Jimbo never fought after that day, but I can tell you we never fought at Ma Essary's house again. And to this day if you told me and Jimbo that Ma Essary was cutting switches, we'd both either take off runnin' or straighten right up or both, and we're both grown men with kids of our own.

PLAYIN' 'POSSUM

For those of you who may not have had the pleasure of meeting an opossum (pronounced 'possum, the o being silent) just imagine a very large whitish-gray rat with a bad case of the mange. They are not the least bit cute, and when cornered they will either bear their teeth and hiss like an old alley cat, or they will lie perfectly still in the hope that you will think they are graveyard dead and go away.

Now Ma Essary's house was a big ole frame structure built up on cinderblocks with a nice big crawl space under it. Around to the back was an opening Poppa Ebb kept a board over to keep the skunks, 'possums, and other varmints out. From time to time, when we were younger me and Jimbo would ease the board back and skinny under the house to listen in on what the adults were talkin' about. The first time, being pure accident, was about the time I turned nine. Ma Essary's ole calico cat had a bunch of kittens hid somewhere, and Jimbo heard someone say a male calico was worth a lot of money, so, of course, we had to go looking for them babies. We didn't find them but crawlin' around up under the house we overheard Momma and Aunt Mae discussin' our Christmas presents with Ma Essary. After that, whenever we wanted to know something, or sometimes just for fun, we'd crawl up under the house and listen in.

The summer after I turned twelve, Momma hollered out the back door for me. It was one of those lazy days and I'd set an old board across the burn barrel. Now, for those of you who did not have the pleasure of being raised redneck, a burn barrel is just what it sounds like, an old metal barrel us country folks use to burn trash. I'd placed three burnt, rusty, tin cans on it, backed up twenty yards, and was trying to knock the cans off by throwing rocks at them. Two of those cans had already fallen when Momma called. I heaved the stone in my hand, missed by a mile, and hurried inside.

"Ma Essary called," Momma said gathering up her purse, "Something's dead over there and she needs our help finding it."

"If'n it's dead why does it need finding?" I wanted to know.

Momma looked at me like I was six kinds of stupid. I thought it was a logical question, so I just kept staring back at her. Finally, realizing I wanted an answer, she shrugged and said, "Because it's stinkin' up her whole house," and headed for the front door.

When we got there, Aunt Mae and Ma Essary were standing on the front porch discussing the probability of it being a stray cat.

"Jimbo is already up under the house. Your Poppa Ebb is around back there with him," Ma Essary pointed around the side of the house, "Harold, you go see if you can give them a hand."

Now, I've never been squeamish and dead things don't bother me much, but for something to really get to smellin', it has to be fairly far along in the process of decay, so I was in no hurry to crawl around up under the house looking for what was left of some stray animal. Lucky for me, about the time I rounded the corner of the house, Jimbo was crawlin' out from under the house with a flashlight in one hand and an empty moonshine jug in the other.

He sported his usual grin as he held up the jug. "This is the only thing I could find under the house."

"Well damn," Poppa Ebb swore, "Guess it must be up in the attic. Least ways, I hope it is. It'll sure as hell be a mess if'n it's in one of the walls."

A quick trip to the barn produced an old wooden ladder, and a stop at the tool shed netted me a flashlight. The smell was rank and strong when I stepped through the back door and into the kitchen and it came right close to makin' me lose my breakfast.

"The crawl hole is at the back of the hallway." Poppa Ebb said from the back porch. I looked over my shoulder as he pulled the door shut. Jimbo stood just inside the door, the usual stupid grin on his face, holding the ladder and looking like the smell had no effect on him. Me, I was thinkin' Poppa Ebb was awful mean to send us in there by ourselves, but maybe, also a bit of a genius.

We found the crawl hole, and I held the ladder, so Jimbo could get up into the attic. Now the attic was unfinished. For those of y'all who have never been in an unfinished attic, there is no flooring. You have to navigate around by balancing on the edge of two-by-six wooden beams. Nailed to the bottom of the beams is the sheetrock so the only thing between you and the room below is one misstep and a thin layer of drywall. By the time I managed to pull myself up and get my flashlight on, Jimbo was scampering around like an overgrown Spider monkey at home in the jungle.

I got my balance, and since Jimbo seemed to be headed for the back of the house, I began the precarious job of making my way to the front. Here and there some critter had used the roll insulation for a nest or just moved it out of the way for whatever reason. I checked each of these with care before moving on. Just as I reached the front wall of the house, Jimbo hollered from the far back corner.

"I think I found the problem." he shouted.

"What is it?" I shouted back.

"Come and see." He hollered.

It made no sense to me for both of us to have to mess with whatever was dead back there, and I started say so, but as I turned back towards the middle of the house, Jimbo hollered again, "Harold, get your ass back here. You gotta see this."

"Awright," I said, moving along as fast as I could without stepping through the sheetrock. I could just imagine the hell Ma Essary would give me if I put a foot through her ceiling.

When I finally got to him, he was perched with both feet on a two-by-six ceiling joist holding on to a rafter with his left hand. On the insulation in front of him was what remained of a squirrel and the carcass of an 'possum. They lay nose to nose, and the smell was enough to knock you down. I squatted down across from Jimbo and wished I'd have thought to bring up a bag to put them in. I was figurin' on how to talk Jimbo into carrying them down out of the attic when he looked up at me.

"You reckon, the squirrel got poisoned and died and then the 'possum came along and was munchin' on the squirrel and got himself poisoned and died too?" he asked.

As usual, my thought process and Jimbo's were miles apart. I shrugged, not really caring how either of the rodents had got dead and bloated up like roadkill on a hot mornin'. I moved the beam of my flashlight from their remains back towards the crawl hole while Jimbo just kept studyin' on them animals.

"I reckon I'll hold the light, so you can carry them out of here," I said like I was just trying to be sensible, "Grab 'em by their tails and let's get goin'."

"Ain't damn likely." Jimbo shook his head as he looked up at me for the first time. "I ain't carrying them both. You grab one and I'll take the other."

"Come on now," I said, "It'll be safer if one of us carries them while the other holds the light."

"Awright," Jimbo returned, "I'll hold the light."

Now when Jimbo gets his back up, it takes a whole lot of negotiatin' or the promise of cash to change his mind. Standing in that stuffy old attic with the temperature risin' and the smell strong enough to wither a person's nose hairs, I figured I just didn't have that much time, so I offered him five dollars.

"Make it ten and we've got a deal." He countered.

After two more rounds of negotiation, we settled on six dollars and twenty-five cents. Jimbo shoved his light into his back pocket, reached down and grabbed the squirrel's tail, and picked it up. I pointed my flashlight, so the light was directly on the 'possum's tail. Jimbo laid the squirrel down arranging it alongside the 'possum so he could grab both of their tails in one hand and still have a hand to hold onto the rafters.

With a good grasp on both tails, he stood up with the varmints in hand, and I stood up with my flashlight pointin' the way to the crawl hole. Just as I was about to turn towards the open space that 'possum went to wiggling and hissing and trying to crawl up Jimbo's arm. Jimbo let loose of it and the squirrel and stepped back—right into the space between two ceiling joists.

One second, he was standing there, the next he was falling through the sheetrock. Off balance myself, I rocked back and forth and watched him fall. I grabbed at empty air and then managed to lay hold of one of the two-by six rafters. Somehow, Jimbo managed to grab a ceiling joist and hold on. As light poured into the attic from the gaping hole his body had made, the 'possum made a mad scramble back into the attic, but the remains of Mr. Squirrel fell with a sickening, squishy sound to the hardwood floor below.

When I finally found my balance, I swung the light around to the 'possum, who was hunched up like a rabid, demon cat hissing at Jimbo like it was going to attack him at any second. Jimbo stared back wide-eyed and hung on to that joist for dear life.

"Do something." He finally whispered through clenched teeth.

"Like what?" I whispered back, wondering why in the hell we were whispering since the damn thing was right there and could hear us perfectly.

I don't know if it was the whispering or the way Jimbo was staring at it, but something set the 'possum off and it turned on me. Now, I'd been around long enough to know 'possums are more bark than bite, but when you are in an enclosed space all such knowledge just seems to go out the window, so when Mr. Possum feigned a jump at me, I started scootin'. I'm not saying 'possums are smart enough to read, but this one must have heard somewhere that if you get the enemy on its heels, it's best to advance, because the second I stepped back onto the next joist, he jumped two feet in my direction.

Jimbo, in his infinite wisdom, decided to try to help and swung both feet up in an attempt to kick the ceiling out from under the 'possum. I won't say it was a completely idiotic decision, or even that I might not have tried it myself in the heat of the moment. The problem was his legs were longer than planned and as I tried to step back to the next joist his feet came through the sheetrock and collided with my foot before it could find the beam. Off balance, I tried to get my foot back to the original joist and failed. Just as my head passed the ceiling joist as I descended through the sheetrock, my eyes locked on those of that 'possum's. I swear he was smiling.

I missed the joist but managed to grab Jimbo's legs on the way down. He squealed and I guess that varmint decided since it had taken me out, Jimbo would be no problem, so it jumped at Jimbo's exposed face. Jimbo let go of the wooden beam and grabbed the 'possum in both hands. I hit the floor first, followed closely by Jimbo, who landed full force on top of me, screaming and fighting the 'possum, that was screaming just as loud and hissing and fighting back.

All of the commotion caused Ma Essary to open the front door and as soon as that varmint saw light and could get shed of Jimbo, he made a streak for it. I was laid out on the floor and tryin' to catch my breath, when that devil rodent charged at Ma Essary with a full head of steam. In an attempt to get out of its way, Ma Essary, Aunt Mae, and Momma all tripped over each other and every one of them landed flat out on their backsides on the porch. Over top of them, I could see Poppa Ebb who was just coming up the front steps. I guess Mr. Possum figured he wasn't as tough as Poppa Ebb, because at the last minute he made a hard right, jumped through the porch railing, and headed across the yard. Poppa Ebb doubled over with laughter at the sight of those three women rolling around on the porch. As my breath came back, all I found myself wondering was why Poppa Ebb had left the back porch and come around front. Ain't it weird how our minds work? Like where Poppa Ebb was and why mattered one heap at that moment.

With Poppa Ebb supervising and Ma Essary fussing constantly, me and Jimbo managed to patch the ceiling the following week. It took most of the next week to find and stop up all the holes in the eave of the house to ensure no further varmints would cause such trouble. To this day neither Jimbo nor I much care for 'possums.

UNCLE THAD

As ornery as my cousin Jimbo is, he can't hold a candle to Uncle Thaddeus. Being Ma Essary's youngest brother, he's actually my great-uncle. I reckon he stands about six-foot-five and weighs in at a solid two-hundred pounds. Just looking at him most folks see a long lanky beanpole of a fella and would never guess he was strong as an Angus bull. They would be wrong. I once saw him take a horseshoe and bend it in on itself with his bare hands.

We didn't see much of him growing up, but the times he was around were sure enough memorable. Ma Essay said he was a ramblin' man. When I asked Pa what that meant, he said, it was someone who wandered around the country and never put down no roots. It sounded kinda fun to me.

'Round about the summer I turned thirteen, Uncle Thaddeus came blowing into town out of the blue one evening. Momma and Sis had just finished clearing the dinner table when the phone rang. When she hung up, Momma said Ma Essary figured we ought to get on over to her place and visit with Uncle Thaddeus, since there was never any telling how long he'd be around. So, me and Pa left them to do the dishes and headed out to do evening chores. When we got back, I crawled into the bed of Pa's old truck, Momma and Sis loaded up with Pa in the cab, and we headed over to Ma Essary's house.

When we got there, Poppa Ebb and Uncle Thaddeus were on the front porch passing a quart jar of Poppa's homemade apple moonshine back and forth and swapping stories. At the sound of the truck doors, Ma Essary stepped to the screen door and hollered for Momma and Sis to come help her with the baking.

Ma Essary always seemed to bake more when Uncle

Thaddeus was around. When I was younger, I thought it was to try and keep him from leaving, now I figure it was just so she didn't have to spend as much time around him.

As soon as the women disappeared into the house, Uncle Thaddeus turned to Pa and grinned, "How's it hangin', Slim."

"Slightly to the right." Pa grinned back and they both chuckled. Now Pa is about the most strait-laced fella you'd ever want to meet, but Uncle Thaddeus seems to bring out a whole other side of him. As a matter of fact, I've noticed Uncle Thaddeus does that with just about everyone he meets.

"How you doin', Harold?" he asked me.

"Alright." I answered.

"Alright," he echoed, "Just alright?"

I just grinned but didn't say anything more.

After a few seconds, Uncle Thad turned his attention back to the older men, pointed at me, and said, "Why I remember when I was this lad's age, I can tell you right now," he said and winked at my Pa. "I was more than alright—I sure was. Why I remember this one little old gal. I reckon she was 'bout two or three years older'n me and…" he went off on a tale that Ma Essary and my mama sure wouldn't have wanted me to hear.

That's how Uncle Thaddeus was. Always had a story and always found a way to tell it. Along about sundown, he was still going strong. Poppa Ebb and Pa had spent most of the evening just listening to him and laughing, when Ma Essary came through the front door with Momma and Sis in tow.

"Y'all better let these folks get on home," she said to Poppa Ebb and Uncle Thaddeus, but she was looking right at Uncle Thaddeus, "Slim has to work tomorrow, and The Revival starts tomorrow evening."

"What revival?" Uncle Thaddeus wanted to know.

"Well, that would be The Second Annual All Faith Christian Holy Ghost Tent Revival held down by the pavilion at the creek." Ma Essary's tone was a little snippy, "And if you were around more often, you might know these things."

"Well, la-teee-da," Uncle Thaddeus shot back as he cocked his head off to one side, "Two years running makes it an annual event, huh?"

"That's right," Ma Essary's tone was pure surly by now, "And if'n you had an ounce of decency in you, you wouldn't be questioning the Spirit."

"You wound me, sister." Uncle Thad said as he leaned back and grabbed his chest in mock pain, then sat back up and added, "You're right, maybe I oughta plan on attendin' just to get my spirit right." Then he shot a wink over my way.

Poppa Ebb had just takin' a drink from the mason jar and before he could swallow it, he laughed so hard it came out his nose. "Thaddeus at a revival, that'll be the day," he said between sputtering and coughing.

Ma Essary stretched to her full height, both hands on her hips, daggers shooting from her eyes, and snarled, "Ebb Essary. You and Thaddeus Joseph can both go to hell." And then in a somewhat softer tone, she turned to Momma, "Now y'all better get on home. See y'all tomorrow." And she stomped across the porch and into the house, slamming the screen door behind her.

Poppa Ebb and Uncle Thad roared with laughter, both of them slapping their knees. Then Uncle Thad started singing "Shall We Gather at The River" in his big baritone voice. Pa started to join in but a look from Momma made him think twice. We could hear Poppa Ebb and Uncle Thad still singing when we were a block away.

* * * * *

I never understood why it was necessary to have the revival in a tent down on the creek when we had six different perfectly good church buildings in our little town, but then what did I know, I was just a kid who hadn't even been dunked in the water yet—much to Momma's dismay. Pa said when it was time I'd know it, and that I just didn't know yet. As I followed Pa down the path to the old tent, I saw Aunt Mae and Uncle Mooney ducking through the opening that served as the door. Aunt Mae had her Bible in one hand, and the other hand was tangled in the back of Jimbo's shirt hustling him along.

Inside Ma Essary was seated three rows back from the front. Somehow, Mrs. Beatrice Merriweather had beat Ma Essary to the revival and laid claim to the first two rows. That wasn't goin' to set well with Ma since she liked to be right up front. Our family, along with Ma Essary and Aunt Mae's crew filled up the entire third row. I managed to find a seat next to Jimbo, and amidst the glares and the warnings from both Momma and Aunt Mae the two of us began to fidget around on the hard wooden fold-up chairs. Once everyone was seated, I noticed that Ma Essary seemed to be trying to stare a hole in the back of Mrs. Merriweather's head and couldn't help but wonder if this revival was going to do her any good at all.

Suddenly the hum of conversation ceased, and the tent went completely silent. When I turned my attention to the front, a short, plump bald man in a black three-piece suit had stepped to the very edge of the stage. He held an old worn Bible in his hands and with a flourish lifted it above his head, "We will bow our heads in prayer. Lord, we are gathered here tonight to do your work…" he cleared his throat like something was caught in it, "We are gathered here to rebuke that ole serpent Satan," he cleared his throat again, and continued. Seemed to me like a good shot of Poppa Ebb's moonshine would have gotten rid of the whatever was botherin' his throat. Each time he cleared his throat, his voice raised an octave and he stretched up on his tip-toes as if trying to hand that Bible to the good Lord himself, "we are gonna evict the devils and demons plaguing these poor sinners…"

Momma always insisted that we bow our heads and close our eyes during prayers, but right around then Jimbo gave me a poke in the side and my eyes popped open. When I looked, he was pointing back over his shoulder at something behind us.

It was Uncle Thaddeus.

On the way from the house to the revival, I'd heard Momma telling Pa how Ma Essary was mad enough to chew tin cans into nails and spit them at Poppa Ebb and Uncle Thaddeus. Seems they'd broken out a quart of Poppa's moonshine right after breakfast and spent the whole day on the front porch cussin', discussin' and drinkin'. By the time Ma Essary got dinner on the table and headed out for the revival, the two of them were working on their fourth bottle of shine.

Now here he came walking down the center isle all dressed up in his best Sunday-go-to-church suit and grinning from ear to ear. He slid into an empty seat two rows back of us and held a finger up to his mouth to let us know that he didn't want Ma Essary to know he was there. As he settled into his chair, I noticed Poppa Ebb standing at the back of the tent just inside the door flap. He, unlike Uncle Thaddeus, was still in his overalls and I could see the bronze ring on the top of a bottle of shine peeking out of one of his pockets.

I barely managed to get turned back around and shut my eyes before the preacher finished up the prayer. Still holding the Bible above his head, he gave it a couple of shakes and said, "Let us begin by singing 'Shall We Gather at the River'."

My Pa tried to suppress a chuckle but did not succeed and so tried to cover it with a cough. Momma wasn't buying it and shot him one of her famous looks. It was taking all the effort I could muster not to turn around and look at Uncle Thaddeus and Poppa Ebb. By the time we finished singing "Shall We Gather at the River" everyone was standing and waving their arms in the air. A couple of women had already started talking in different languages. Last year, I asked Pa where they were from and didn't they know English? He told me they were from around town and it wasn't exactly a foreign language, they called it 'talkin' in tongues'. When I asked Poppa Ebb about it, he just laughed and said given the right spirits he sometimes talked in tongues too. I found that kind of funny at the time cause I'd never seen Poppa anywhere near a church.

Next, we sang "That Old Time Religion" followed by "Jesus Hold My Hand" and then "There's a Better Day Comin'". There was no pause between songs. When one finished, the preacher would start right into the next one and with each new song the frenzy grew until the air around me seemed to be electrified. All of a sudden, a lady who was sittin' two seats down from Mrs. Merriweather started screaming and moaning and quivering and then just fainted clean away. Lucky for her the fella right next to her grabbed hold of her before she smacked her head on the edge of the stage. I looked over at Jimbo, and he was grinning from ear to ear and was just a jumpin' and a shoutin' and havin' the best time.

As soon as we finished singing the last hymn, the preacher's hand shot from above his head straight out at the crowd. I remember thinkin' it was a miracle he didn't lose hold of the Good Book and chunk it right out amongst us. Once again, he raised way up on his tiptoes, and started to quiver all over and I began to fear he was gonna keel over like the young lady in the front row, only there was no one up there to catch him if he did.

"I can feel the Spirit !!!" he shouted, "Can you feel the Spirit?!!!"

Someone behind us shouted, "Yes, Lord, Oh Lord, yes, I can feel the Spirit!!"

"Someone needs healin'!!!" the preacher punctuated each word with a thrust of his Bible, "I can feel it!! Someone out there needs some healin'!! Oh, Lord!! Amen and Hallelujah!!! Who needs healin'?!!!"

Me and Jimbo started lookin' around tryin' to figure out who it was and hopin' it wasn't us, when a man stood up from the back row waving one hand above his head and holding his other arm up against his body. That arm looked funny, all twisted up somehow. He stepped into the aisle right in front of Poppa Ebb and shouted, "It's me!! Oh Lord, help this sinner!! I need healin'!!!"

All heads turn to the back of the tent. I was so excited about seein' that man get healed, I thought I was gonna wet myself. Then, just as the man with the bad arm started to take a step up the aisle, Poppa Ebb reached out a foot and tripped him. To keep from planting face first into the ground, he stretched out both arms and caught himself.

"It's a miracle!!" Poppa Ebb shouted as he helped him to his feet.

I cut my eyes around to Ma Essay and she was just standing, mouth hanging open, eyes wide, and face as red as her famous cherry tomatoes. Before she or anyone else could react, Uncle Thaddeus stepped into the isle.

"It is I, Lord!!" he wailed and stepped up to the edge of the stage, "It is I. I am the sinner you are lookin' for, Lord!! Help me!! Heal me!!"

"Oh, Brother," the preacher wailed with him, "What is it that ails you?!!"

"Vile spirits!!," Uncle Thaddeus wailed louder and started to shake all over like he was 'bout to have a seizure, "Vile spirits!! Demons and devils and the likes!! Oh, help me, Lord!!"

And the preacher reached out with his free hand and grabbed Uncle Thaddeus by the head and started shaking it and his Bible and shrieking, "Oh, Brother, tell me brother, what is it these evil spirits make you do?!!"

"Oh, Preacher," Uncle Thaddeus' knees began to wobble, and I was afraid he was on his way down, "Oh, preacher, they make me drink vile liquor. That evil and disgusting moonshine. Help me preacher, help me." And threw his hands up in the air moaning and wailing.

"Let me heal you, brother," Preacher shouted back and begin to move Uncle Thaddeus' head round and round in big circles while still waving his Bible up in the air, "Let me…"

Uncle Thaddeus interrupted, "And brother, they tell me to fornicate. Oh, brother, they make me do great and wonderful things to women. Not just one, brother, but many. They make me pleasure women all around this country. It is a curse. A beam in my eye. A plank in my groin. Can you heal me, preacher, can you heal me?"

"I can heal you brother," the preacher pushed Uncle

Thaddeus' head round faster and faster until I feared he was gonna tear it clean off, then suddenly he stopped moving it, let loose of it, and held his hand out just inches from Uncle Thaddeus forehead, "Vile spirits, demons from hell, you have no power here!!" he screamed, "I evict you from this man!! Be gone you devils, be gone!!" and with grand flurry he switched hands and slapped Uncle Thaddeus square in the forehead with his Bible.

Uncle Thaddeus stumbled back a couple of steps, started quivering all over, and then his eyes closed, and he started to sway. I just knew he was gonna pass out, but then he slowly started to turn in a circle still trembling. When he had turned so that he was facing Ma Essary, his eyes shot open so wide I thought he was actually possessed. Then he flashed her a quick grin and wink, and let those eyes roll right back up into his head and started chanting in an ear-wrenching high-pitched voice. When I could finally tear my eyes away, I looked back at Jimbo and he was dancin' and squealin' just like a little version of Uncle Thaddeus. I was beginning to think if this was what happened when a fella got the spirit, then I might not ever want to get it.

Looking back towards Uncle Thaddeus, I noticed that Ma Essary's hands had dropped to her sides, and she was stiff as an old board. I thought for a second maybe she was gonna get the spirit too, but she never did. Instead, Uncle Thaddeus stopped vibrating around in a circle, stood quaking for an instant, and then dropped like a rock to the ground. All six-foot five inches of him, just laid out there on the ground.

Ma Essary stepped out into the aisle. I thought maybe she was gonna check on him but instead she just walked right by and headed towards the back of the tent with Momma and Aunt Mae right behind her. Pa and Uncle Mooney hustled me and Jimbo out into the aisle. Pa reached down and got ahold of Uncle Thaddeus under one arm and Uncle Mooney grabbed him under the other and they started for the rear. At the exit, Poppa Ebb held the flap back and with Uncle Thad's heels cutting grooves into the ground, they hauled him all the way to Poppa Ebb's truck.

I don't recall how everyone ended up at Ma Essary's but we did. I do remember that Ma Essary refused to come out of the house and threatened to shoot Uncle Thaddeus if he came through the front door. To prove she was serious, she was standing in the middle of the living room with Poppa's double-barrel shotgun trained on the door when the menfolk arrived.

The woman all gathered up in the kitchen and pouted and cussed Uncle Thaddeus, and Poppa Ebb, and men in general, while all the men and me and Jimbo sat around the front porch. Poppa Ebb pulled the moonshine out of his overall pocket and Uncle Thaddeus kept the stories coming deep into the night.

After that night, we didn't see Uncle Thaddeus again until we laid Poppa Ebb to rest. And even then, Ma Essary wouldn't let him in the house or speak to him. Thinkin' back on that night, I'm pretty sure Uncle Thaddeus never really got the spirit, and I'm damn sure Ma Essary lost any spirit she might have had. That's not to say, she didn't find it again later, but I reckon it may have taken quite a while.

COBRAS & RATTLESNAKES

Cobras and rattlesnakes. Those are the only two types of snakes that I know of. Now, some folks will try to tell you differently. They will even try to tell you that some snakes are not dangerous at all, but Poppa Ebb, me, and Jimbo know better. It's really pretty simple, if it has a rattle, it's a rattlesnake. If it doesn't have a rattle, it's a cobra. And the sight of these slithering demons will cause a sane man to hurt himself just trying to get away; therefore, all snakes are dangerous.

So, when I got a call from Jimbo sayin' we needed to go to Ma Essary's and help her with a snake problem, I wanted badly to refuse. Nowadays I'd simply lie and tell him I was running trotlines on the Washita and would get there as soon as I could, but this all happened before cellphones, so Jimbo knew I was a quarter of a mile away in my trailer. I hung up the phone, started pacin' around the living room, trying to find a reason I could use to call him back and say I couldn't make it. My keys were on the table next to the door, and I seriously considered throwing them into the woods behind my house, but then I couldn't figure out how I would get to work the next morning. Plus, I figured Jimbo was as skeerd—that's the redneck word that means you're way beyond just plain old afraid and have likely even jumped right past terrified—of snakes as I was, so he'd probably just run over and pick me up.

In the end, I wandered into the bedroom and dressed for the occasion. Now, I spend some time in the woods, hunting and fishing and what-not, so I know how to dress in the months when the snakes are most likely to be out and about, but this one according to Jimbo was inside Ma Essary's house. I found myself in a bit of a dilemma. Should I dress like I would in the woods, or just put on my regular go-to-grandma's house clothes. After careful consideration, I decided not to take any chances and dressed for the woods, and since I figured to be in some pretty close quarters with said snake, I decided it would be best to add a few extra precautionary items.

When I stepped out onto the front porch, I had my camouflage snake guards strapped on over the top of my steel-toed work boots. My blue, wind pants had a one-inch white stripe down the side and were stuffed deep into my leather Wolverines. It being mid-July the only long-sleeved shirt I could find quickly was a red and white flannel number. I had grabbed my heavy Carhart coat off the rack on my way out the door, and by the time I made it to my truck, I could already feel the sweat running down my back and along the side of my ribs.

Five minutes later, I arrived at Ma Essary's to find Poppa Ebb sittin' in his favorite chair on the front porch with his single-shot twenty-gauge shotgun broke open across his knees and a tall glass of shine in his hand. I grabbed up my leather work gloves and the Carhart as I got out of the truck.

"Where's the snake, Poppa?" I asked him as I pulled on the heavy coat.

"Guest room," he gave a snort of disgust with his answer, took a sip of shine, and added, "she says it's Bob. I told her I didn't give a damn if it was Saint Michael himself, if she didn't have it out of the house in thirty minutes, I was gonna blow it's durn head clean off."

"Oh, come on now Poppa." I said as I pulled my gloves on.

He took another sip, then looked me up and down, took the gold pocket watch out of the breast pocket of his bibbed overall, and said, "You've got twelve minutes left, Captain America."

Leaving him on the porch, I eased the screen door back, checked to make sure all was clear in the living room, and stepped quickly into the house. The screen door slammed close behind me, and I nearly shit my drawers.

"Dammit Ebb it ain't been thirty minutes." Ma Essary screamed from around the corner and down the hall.

"It's Harold," I yelled back, "sorry about the door."

"Dang it, Harold," Jimbo's voice floated down the hall, "I dang near messed my pants."

I didn't tell him that I had nearly done the same but stepped around the corner and plastered myself to the wall. Twenty feet away at the far end of the hall was Ma Essary, and she motioned for me to come on. I eased down toward her with both hands against the sheetrock. Standing there beside her, sweating like I'd run a mile, I was starting to feel a little foolish and overdressed.

Ma Essary pulled at my coat sleeve as she stepped away from the door. "Why don't you step around me, so you can see into the room?"

I had no desire to be any closer to the room, but before I could say so, she shoved me right to the edge of the door frame. I stuck my head just far enough around to see Jimbo. He was standing in the middle of the queen-size guest bed. His snake guards were tan and strapped over his black snake-skin cowboy boots. He had his camouflage hunting pants tucked into them and bloused out, so if the snake struck it would hit the pants and not get his leg. His long-sleeved shirt was a blue Wrangler work shirt and he'd left it hanging out over his pants. Even though Ma Essary didn't usually allow anything on one's head in the house, he had on his old sweat-stained black Stetson cowboy hat. I felt a bit better about the ensemble I'd chosen for the night's party.

"Get your ass in here," he growled when he saw me looking at him.

"Why?" I asked. It seemed like a logical question.

He gave me a disgusted look. "Cause I don't want to be in here by myself."

"Why?" I asked. It seemed like a logical follow-up question.

"Cause there's a snake in here." He returned.

"What kind of snake?" I asked.

"I only saw its tail when it crawled under the bed earlier," he answered, "It didn't have a rattler."

"So, it's a cobra." I said and he nodded.

"It is not." Ma Essary's tone held a good degree of disgust, "It's Bob from my garden. He's a harmless ole rat snake."

"Ain't no such thing as a harmless snake." Jimbo argued, "And this one is a cobra."

"Well in that case, I really don't want to come in there." I told him.

"Dammit, Harold." Jimbo whined.

Ma Essary gave me another shove and ordered, "Get in there."

Now, I didn't know for sure whether that slithering critter was under the bed when she pushed me and I wasn't exactly prepared, so instead of just stepping into the room, I tried to jump sideways across the six feet of hardwood and land on the bed. It was not a good idea. I did manage to get both feet on the edge of the bed, but it gave under my weight and dumped me right in the middle of the floor.

Ma Essary uses the guest room for storage more often than she does for visitors, and from my position on the floor, I could see the stacks of shoe boxes she had filled with stuff and stored up under the bed. I was wondering what in the world Ma Essary had stored in all those boxes when Bob stuck his head up from between two of them, and we locked eyes. He stuck his tongue out, hissed, and drew back to strike. At least that's what I think he was plannin'. You can never be sure about cobras. I went to scramblin' sideways and tryin' to get my feet under me. When I finally stopped, I was back out in the hallway, and Jimbo was down on his hands and knees in the middle of that bed.

"Dang Harold, you darn near knocked me off the bed," he complained.

"I... I seen... I seen him." I stammered.

Jimbo pushed himself up to a standing position once again, looked at me, and started to laugh. "Man, you should have seen your face when you hit the floor." He held his side and talked through the laughter, "and the way you moved tryin' to get shut of that snake. That was classic. Funny as hell."

"Oh, yeah," I could feel the red creeping up my neck, "Maybe I'll just go out front with Poppa Ebb and leave you to it."

He quit laughing instantly, "Aw, come on, Harold," he started in beggin'.

My first step into the room took me halfway to the bed. Jimbo threw out a hand to help me. I leaped the last few feet and grabbed it. He hauled me up into the bed, and we stood back-to-back, swaying and circling, and looking over the edge of the bed, trying to catch a look at Bob.

"You think he's still under...?" Jimbo pointed down and spoke in a whisper.

"I don't know." I wasn't sure why we were whispering.

Sometime in the past, Poppa Eb had found a bunch of metal shop shelves at a garage sale and bought them. He'd brought them home and mounted them to two of the walls in the guest room so Ma Essary would have more storage. I suddenly realized that the snake could be just about anywhere. Looking around the various stuff stacked on those shelves, my eyes came across a set of old encyclopedias. Why those books caught my eye, I don't know, but I suddenly had a desire to grab the "S" volume and see if I could figure out where snakes liked to hide.

"Maybe we should flip the mattress off the bed and see if it's still under it." Jimbo suggested.

I looked at him, then at the wrinkled comforter we were standing on. "Just how do you plan to do that with us standin' in the middle of it?"

He narrowed his eyes into slits. He leaned from one side of the bed to the other and I realized he was studying on it. After a minute of silence, he finally said, "We'll get down on our knees on the bed facing the wall and then just rear back. Our weight will pull it up and over the edge and we'll be behind it. We'll be shielded from the snake."

I had some serious doubts about the plan, but couldn't come up with a better one, so we hollered at Ma Essary, who'd disappeared up the hall. A minute later, we heard her coming back.

She peeked around the corner of the door. "What ch'all want?"

"Take a look in here and see if you see it on your side of the bed." Jimbo told her.

She took a quick look around the doorframe, and then pulled her head back. "I don't see him. I'll be right back. I'm goin' to the kitchen and find something to hold Bob's head down when y'all do find him."

When she left, we took up positions facing the back wall like Jimbo suggested. On Jimbo's order, we heaved as hard as we could. Now, I'm pretty sure on a regular day there is no way we could get that mattress up and over, but this was no normal day, and our adrenaline was flowin' kinda high, so it came up and over on the first try. As soon as our feet hit the floor, we shoved one edge of the mattress up against the wall. Neither of us could see over the top, so Jimbo held it still, and I slipped to the other end and looked around it. I saw dozens and dozens of boxes. A couple of pairs of ladies high-heel shoes and a lone white tube sock were wedged between the boxes near the middle of the bed, but the snake was nowhere in sight.

"Ain't there," I told Jimbo, "Might as well drop the mattress back down."

As soon as the mattress hit the frame, we were off the floor and back in the middle of the bed. The comforter and sheet were now in one big ball in the middle of it. Ma Essary stuck her head around the corner and then tossed a spaghetti ladle and a back scratcher across the room and onto the bed. Me and Jimbo just stood there looking at them.

"What are we supposed to do with these?" Jimbo asked.

"When you see the snake, use them to hold his head down while I get a pillowcase and we'll put him in it. I think we can get him out of the house like that." She explained.

Jimbo grabbed the ladle and left the back scratcher for me. This did not seem like a good plan to me, but then I had been wrong about flipping the mattress, so who was I to say. I picked up the back scratcher and hoped that the thing would really hold a cobra's head down long enough to get it into a pillowcase.

Once again, me and Jimbo got into our back-to-back position and started circling. About the fourth time around, my eyes fell on those dang encyclopedias again and there was Bob. At least there was his head. His body was hidden somewhere behind the books, but his head was laid right up across the D volume, and he had his beady little eyes on me and Jimbo. I froze and Jimbo sensing something was up, froze too.

"I got him." I said barely loud enough to be heard.

"Where?" Jimbo whispered without moving.

"Bookshelf. Encyclopedia. Volume D." I answered.

"D. Demon." Jimbo turned in slow motion, "It's a sign."

I shook my head. Bob must have realized he'd been spotted because just about then he pulled his head back and disappeared completely behind the books. The plastic back scratcher I had in my hand was about two feet long and had a hand at the end with the fingers bent like a person would bend theirs to scratch. I had grabbed it up without taking a close look at it but now I realized it would be very useful in pulling the books off the shelf so we could get at that durn snake. I told Jimbo to grab ahold of my wrist and I'd hold onto his, so I could lean out and reach the books without getting off the bed.

By doing this, I was able to reach the top of the volumes. Stretching out as far as I could, I placed the plastic finger on the D volume, squeezed down on the handle of the scratcher, and something buzzed like the buttons vibrating on a rattle snake. Jimbo jerked me back to safety. I dropped the back scratcher, and the sound stopped.

My poor old heart was beating a hundred miles an hour. "I thought you said it didn't have a rattle."

Jimbo threw up his hands. "It didn't, I swear."

"It was the scratcher." Ma Essary's voice came from the hallway, and it sounded like she was laughing.

"What?" I asked.

45

"The back scratcher," she said with half a giggle. "It's battery powered. I thought the batteries were dead. I guess I was wrong."

"You think!" The sarcasm in my voice caused Ma Essary to stick her head around the corner. If old Bob had seen the look she gave me, he would have withered up and died right there behind those encyclopedias.

Jimbo saved me, bless his heart. "Ma Essary, I think we need something longer. Maybe the hoe would work."

"It's dark and the hoe's out in the barn. I'm not going out there. I'll go see what I can find in the utility room," she said and disappeared again.

Without a word of warning, Jimbo jumped off the end of the bed, grabbed the back scratcher, and dived back belly first. I had to grab the headboard to keep from falling. Holding the scratcher up like it was a piece of precious treasure, he crawled to his feet. He handed it back to me and we got back into position. One by one, I pulled the books off the shelf and onto the floor being careful not to push the button again. With each volume, a little bit more of the snake was exposed. He was curled into a ball and except for an occasional flick of the tongue he laid perfectly still.

Volumes A through Q lay on the floor before he was completely exposed. My heart thumped in my chest, and there wasn't a dry spot on my flannel shirt. I raised an eyebrow over at Jimbo as if to ask what we should do next. He just shrugged and held up his spaghetti ladle. Footsteps in the hallway gave us hope.

We turned to the door just in time to see Poppa Ebb step through it. His eyes went to the two of us standing on the bed. I just stood there staring at him, but Jimbo broke eye contact with him and looked at the snake. That's all Poppa Ebb needed. He turned, threw the shotgun to his shoulder, and pulled the trigger. The explosion was deafening. Both me and Jimbo grabbed our ears and dropped to a seated position on the bed.

"Poppa Ebb, you durn near deafened me." Jimbo whined.

"Time's up," he said and calmly walked away.

From up the hall, I could hear Ma Essary's voice. It sounded very faint and far away, but from the tone, I could tell she was not happy, and she was actually screaming something about how that she didn't want Bob killed and if rats got in the house, then Poppa was going to have to catch every one of them with his bare hands. When I looked back to where Bob had been perched beside the R volume, there was a fair size hole in the sheetrock and Bob was in several pieces.

If any of you have any doubts about how dangerous snakes are, I hope this has educated you. There is no such thing as a harmless snake. Even if their bite won't kill you, there is a good chance that physical or mental damage will be caused to someone anytime one of the demon critters is around.

PA'S PECAN PIE

My Pa wasn't a drinkin' man. Now that's not to say he didn't take a snort of whiskey now and then, when the bottle was passed 'round at a family gatherin'. He just wasn't inclined to drink on a daily basis. My cousin Jimbo's dad, Uncle Mooney, was a drinkin' man. Like most of the men on Momma's side of the family, he was of the inclination that if a beer a day kept your kidneys functioning at their optimum levels, then a six pack must be even better.

One thing about redneck gatherings is there is never a lack of alcohol. Both for drinking and, when possible, in the food itself. Aunt Maude's Rum Cake was always present at every holiday and a big hit with the ladies. When Ma Essary's freezer could hold no more catfish, it was beer-battered, fried, and consumed with - you guessed it cold beer.

The Thanksgiving just before I turned eight, Pa talked Momma into putting bourbon into the pecan pies. He'd read about it in some magazine and thought it sounded good.

We arrived at Ma Essary's well before mealtime. Jimbo was waiting in the porch swing for me and, as soon as I got instructions and threats from Momma, we headed around the house to the backyard. At the very back corner of the lot behind Ma Essary's garden at the edge of Poppa Ebb's orchard was a gigantic pecan tree. This was our tree. It was far enough away that the grownups couldn't hear or see us but close enough for us to hear them if they hollered for us.

"Guess what, Harold, I got a new huntin' dawg." Jimbo told me as we found our usual spots and leaned back against the ole tree. The way it had grown up from the ground left two perfect indentations for us to sit in. Each seat had a set of roots running out from the base like the arms on a chair. In our best blue jeans, white button-up the front shirts, and Sunday-go-to-church shoes, I'm sure we looked like perfect little gentlemen just visiting the day away.

"Oh, yeah," I said, "Well we got us a new yella tom cat and he's meaner'n sin."

Jimbo mulled that over for a minute, then asked, "Think he's meaner'n Poppa Ebb's three-legged weiner dawg?"

I rubbed my chin the way I'd seen Pa do when he was thinkin' hard 'bout some problem, "Nah, I don't reckon he's that mean."

We sat quiet for a few minutes just looking out across the pasture and then Jimbo spoke up, "Hey what did y'all bring? We brought some fudge and that pink stuff Ma always makes for Thanksgiving."

"Well, we brought six pecan pies," I told him in my most grown up tone, "and they all have bourbon in them."

"What's bourbon?" he wanted to know.

"It's like beer only different." I repeated what Momma had told me when I asked her.

"Different, how?" came his next question.

"It's a lot like whiskey." I repeated what Pa had told me when I had asked him.

"I gotta idea." Jimbo said as he pushed himself up off the ground.

I stood up and wiped the seat of my breeches off as I listened. Just as Jimbo finished telling me his big idea, Ma Essary hollered from the back porch that the food was on the table, and we'd best get on in the house. Mostly the house seems plenty big, but when the whole clan gets together for holidays the place somehow seems to shrink. We pushed and shoved and gathered up around the table as best we could. When the last of the kinfolks had been accounted for Pa was asked to bless the food. He prayed loud and clear in a big baritone voice that filled the room. When he finished everyone muttered, "Amen," and set about scramblin' for plates.

The older folks gathered round Ma Essary's big dining room table, while the teenagers and such headed for the living room. Anyone under the age of ten was shooed out to the porch with their plate and drink. Jimbo and I claimed the porch swing and set to cleaning our plates of the turkey, ham, mashed potatoes, and dressing, that had been heaped on them. Using a roll, we sopped up the last bit of food and tossed our paper plates in the trash. Smiling like little angels we headed for the desert table set up in the kitchen right next to the back door.

On the way through, Jimbo grabbed a knife and two forks and shoved them in his hip pocket. A quick check to make sure no one was looking, and we each grabbed two of the pecan pies and skedaddled out to our pecan tree. After a brief discussion it was decided we should cut each pie into six pieces, so it would be kinda of like the six packs Uncle Mooney brought home every evening after work.

"You ever been drunk?" Jimbo asked me.

"No, how 'bout you?" I asked in return.

"Nah, but I seen my Pa do it, so I'm pretty sure I know how." He said with a big toothy grin and handed me a fork.

Being new to the experience, I wasn't sure if I should eat it fast or slow, so I just kinda watched Jimbo and kept to his pace. After three pieces, each of us had eaten half of our first pie, and I was starting to fill a little bloated around the middle, but that was about it.

"Now's the tricky part," Jimbo let out an enormous belch and then continued, "Somewhere between four and six beers, Pa usually starts to have trouble walkin' and he don't talk real plain, so if that happens, we'll have to help each other back up to the house."

"Sounds good to me." I said and picked up my fork to start on the next piece of pie.

"You, okay?" Jimbo asked.

"I think so," I answered, "Why, am I doing something wrong?"

"I ain't sure," Jimbo looked me straight in the eyes, "I think I'm startin' to feel it a little. How 'bout you?"

"Well, I feel a little full, but that's about it." I told him.

"O' Lordy," he shook his head, "I hope you ain't no al-key-holic."

"What?" I nearly dropped my fork, "What's that?"

"Well, Ma says it's someone who drinks all the time, but you can never tell it," He explained, "And brother, I hear they're meaner'n sin."

"Well, I ain't no al-key-holic." I told him and went to town on the rest of that pie.

By the time, we'd finished our first pies, both of us were leaned back against the ole pecan tree for support and neither of us could form a complete sentence. Jimbo kept holding his fork up so we could clink them together, but neither of us had the coordination to do it. Every time we missed, it brought on a new bout of laughter.

"Tink I had 'nuf." I slurred.

"Nah," Jimbo smirked, "Have s'more."

"Can't." I tried to stand up, staggered, and grabbed the tree for support.

Jimbo reached up and pulled me back to my seat. "Wimp." He grinned.

Now there it was. Wimp. Like a dare and an insult all in one. I don't know why some words just get under a fella's skin, but they do and when they do, you've gotta prove you don't belong in said category, so I picked up my fork and started on that second pie. Before, I knew it, me and Jimbo had nearly finished the second pies and we were wasted.

"Gotta go." Jimbo looked over at me with eyes glazed over. Now I wasn't sure if he meant he needed a bathroom or if he just wanted to go back to the house, so I used the tree for support and stood up. When I reached down to help him up, I lost my balance and face planted right there in the dirt.

Jimbo somehow crawled over and helped me roll over. I

stared up into his face and suddenly fear like rushing water flooded over me and knew if I didn't get us some help, we were both gonna die. I grabbed him by the shirt and on hands and knees started crawling towards the house with him in tow. Halfway through Ma Essary's garden, I lost hold of Jimbo and knew I didn't have the strength to drag him the rest of the way. He'd passed smooth out and was just too durn heavy to drag any further. Pure will, mixed with unadulterated fear kept me going until I reached the steps of the back porch. My cries for help brought Aunt Maude to the screen door, followed by Ma Essary and then the entire family.

"What in the world?" Ma Essary scrambled down the steps and grabbed me up.

"Pie… Bourbon… Drunk… So… So, Sorry…" I stammered and started to cry. Big tears flowed down my cheeks.

"What's he saying?" my Momma came through the back door frantic and grabbed me from Ma Essary.

"I think he's sayin' him and Jimbo got drunk on your bourbon pecan pies." Ma Essary laughed. I failed to see the humor in the situation but was too far gone to say so.

"But I cooked them, there's no…" Momma started to say, but Ma Essary cut her off with a wave of her hand.

"It's alcohol poisoning," Ma Essary said with a grand gesture of her hands waving everyone back, "I've seen it before. I reckon we better figure something quick or they're both gonna die."

In a haze, I looked around at all my kin. The youngsters looked horrified and some of the little ones had started cryin'. Their mothers started gatherin' them up and takin' them back into the house away from the impending doom. I looked up at the sky and through my tears, for a brief moment, I thought I saw angels floating along with the clouds.

"The hospital's closed for Thanksgiving and all the doctors will be out of town," Aunt Maude chimed in, "What are we going to do?" I could hear her chokin' back the tears.

"I might know a way to save them," Ma Essary said, "It's a long shot, but it might work."

"Tell us, tell us quick." Momma said.

"Mix three raw eggs in a glass with two shots of Tabasco and a dash of cayenne pepper and bring it to me as quickly as possible." She ordered and my Pa rushed back into the house like the devil himself was chasin' after him.

He returned in an instant with the miracle cure and Ma Essary proceeded to pour it down my throat. Somewhere along about then, Uncle Mooney and Pa managed to drag Jimbo out of the garden and lay him down next to the porch. I could see he was beginning to come around, and I was sure hopin' they could get some of the cure into him before he passed over to the other side, when the first swallow of that horrid concoction hit the back of my throat. I managed to get it down, but it came right up and somewhere in the middle of my chest, it met the next bit going down. I durn near choked to death before it all agreed on a direction, and that direction was out. Ma Essary let go of me, and I hit the ground on my hands and knees and proceeded to empty my gut of everything I had eaten in the past week.

About the time the last bit hit the ground, Jimbo came off the ground in a dead run headed for the pasture. I think he would've made it, if he hadn't got tripped up in the dead cucumber vines that Poppa Ebb hadn't plowed under just yet. He went down like a rock and Uncle Mooney dragged him back kickin' and screamin' and swearing he was sober as the Pope.

"What'd ya think?" Uncle Mooney asked Ma Essary.

She held Jimbo's face still and looked deep into his eyes, then squeezed his cheeks, and sniffed his breath. "It's the devil's work," she said, "This boy is surely drunk."

Someone handed her a fresh glass of the miracle cure and between her and Pa and Uncle Mooney, they got most of it down Jimbo's throat. Just like me, he expelled every last bit of his Thanksgiving meal including them two pecan pies. When the grown-ups where right sure we were both gonna live, they wondered back into the house and left us laying out in the yard holding our stomachs and groaning.

I figured at some point they'd come on back out and cut some switches, but they never did. The longer I waited the more I began to think that our near-death miss had scared them so bad that it just wasn't in them to whoop on us.

Later that night, as I was tossing in my bed at home trying to get to sleep, I heard Momma saying something about cooking those pecan pies and asking Pa how it could possibly have affected me and Jimbo so badly. I remember that he chuckled and said, "You never know, darlin'. The mind is a powerful thing."

BARKING TREE FROGS &
LITTLE GREEN ELEPHANTS

Poppa Ebb used to say there are two kinds of people in this world. Those who could laugh at a barking tree frog and those who got upset about the trumpet of a little green elephant. In other words, some folks find passing gas downright funny, and others are offended by it. I can't speak for every redneck, but the ones I grew up around were more inclined to be from the first group. One of Pa's favorite pranks was to wait until you weren't looking, walk up behind you, let one of those silent-but-deadly eggs and orange juice foggers, and then try to slip away before the smell hit your nostrils, leaving you to stare around trying to figure out what just happened.

Poppa Ebb on the other hand was inclined to be more public about it. He'd lift his butt cheek off whatever he was sitting on, let'er rip, and then shout, "Five dollars to anyone who can catch that barking tree frog." When Jimbo turned eight, he finally quit trying to earn that green Lincoln.

Whenever we would have our big family get-togethers if anyone let one rip, and someone always let one rip, someone else would nearly always holler for Uncle Mooney to tell his story. At which time Aunt Mae would go into a full-blown tizzy and declare that story had been told enough. Uncle Mooney would grin his big toothy smile, wave her off with a laugh, clear his throat, and begin.

Some stories begin with 'once upon a time,' but Uncle Mooney always started this story off with, "I reckon, we'd been married all of three weeks on the night in question."

"We'd only been married three days." Aunt Mae would always correct him with her usual scowl.

61

"Now, I gotta tell y'all, Mae here is the love of my life," he would say, "And not just because she's the purtiest gal in the whole county…"

The first time he told the story, Aunt Mae interrupted and said, "in the whole wide world" and so to this day when the story is told, Uncle Mooney pauses and everyone in the whole group, except Aunt Mae, of course, shouts, "In the whole wide world."

"But also, because she is the best damn cook in the whole county," he would go on.

I don't know that Aunt Mae actually caused the next part, but because the story had become a family affair, Uncle Mooney will once again pause so we can all shout, "In the whole wide world."

"When she's of a mind to," Uncle Mooney always winks at her, "She can sure enough lay out a spread and on that day, she done just that. For dinner, she went all out. She cooked up some of her famous glazed pork chops and…"

Uncle Mooney no longer had to pause, the crowd at this point would cut in, "fried potatoes, boiled cabbage, baked beans, and homemade yeast rolls."

With a grin Uncle Mooney then continued, "That's right, and don't forget the cold beer."

Everyone would make a loud popping sound like a beer can opening, and Pa would let loose with a short burst of the old Jim Ed Brown song "Pop A Top Again." When he finished, everyone would make a sound like beer fizzing and Uncle Mooney would continue.

"And for dessert, the best blackberry cobbler I've ever eat, served up with a big ole scoop of French vaniller ice cream." He would rub his big old belly and close his eyes like one of Poppa Ebb's old sows laid up in the mud after cleanin' up the day's slop bucket.

And the crowd would lean in and say, "Mmmmmmm."

"Damn skippy," Uncle Mooney would agree, "Ain't had a pie like that since."

"Ain't likely to ever get another one either." Aunt Mae would always snarl.

"Anyhow," Uncle Mooney ignored her, "I et and et and et, and then you know what I did?"

"No!" we would all play along, "What did you do?"

"Well, what any good husband does when his purty little wife cooks for him," he grinned, "I et some more."

"Then what happened?" We all asked in unison.

"Well, I moseyed on over to my big ole recliner and just laid there and let it all rot," he answered.

"And rot and rot and rot." Everyone had the routine down. Aunt Mae would just shake her head and roll her eyes.

"Yep." Uncle Mooney agreed, "Now unbeknownst to me at the time, Mae here..." he would always give her another wink and she would always blush "... had tossed her birth control pills out and was rearin' to go."

To which we would all shout, "Jimbo."

And Jimbo shouted back, "What?"

And Uncle Mooney would throw up both hands and shake his head. "Hold up."

"Whoa back." We would all yell and lean back in our chairs.

"Let's not get ahead of ourselves," Uncle Mooney would lean in and say, "Will get to Jimbo by and by, but not just yet."

That was always about the time when Aunt Mae would start askin' if anyone needed anything from the kitchen and would try to slip away. Of course, no one ever did, so she fidgeted around, and Uncle Mooney continued with his story.

"Long about dark, I was laid up in my chair waiting for all that food to rot," he would nearly always rub his little round tummy again and then give us all a big wink. "That's when Mae slipped off to the bedroom."

"Just skip to the end this year. Everyone knows this fool story by heart." Aunt Mae would whine.

"No can do," Uncle Mooney would grin, "Can't leave out the best part of the story."

Aunt Mae would give him another one of her looks like she gave me and Jimbo when she was mad. How Uncle Mooney could say another word was a mystery to me, but he didn't miss a beat.

"After, oh, I don't know, maybe a half-hour," he would say, "She hollered at me from the bedroom."

Everyone looked at Aunt Mae, who was sittin' in her rockin' chair all red-faced with pursed lips giving Uncle Mooney a look like she was trying to melt his tongue. Uncle Mooney looked all around the room, but never at Aunt Mae.

"Well, I gathered myself up out of that there chair and ambled on into the bedroom and bless my soul. Mae had gone and bought her one of those fancy frilly neck-la-jay things like in the J.C. Penney's catalog, and she was laid out across the bed just like one of them models. I never seen anything so purty in all my life, and I just stood there with my mouth open, and my jaw resting on my big ole belly." Uncle Mooney would drop his jaw to demonstrate, while Aunt Mae just turned redder and redder.

"Then she patted the edge of the sheet and says for me to come on to bed and called me her big hunk of a lover."

Aunt Mae always interrupted at this point, "I did not say that."

"Well, something like that, and it's close enough, less'n you want me to tell the rest of what you called me," Uncle Mooney would wave his hand and continue. "I don't reckon I've ever gotten outta my overalls that fast before or since. And next thing I know we're all tangled up under them sheets."

"Then what happened," the crowd asked.

"Y'all know what happened." Aunt Mae always snapped at this point.

"Well just about the time things started to get rather serious, if you know what I mean," Uncle Mooney always wiggled his eyebrows at that point, "All that food rottin' down in my gut decided it needed a little extra room to perculate."

"Goodness gracious, Mooney!" Aunt Mae slapped the air in

front of him as if that would shut him up. "I'm sick and tired of you tellin' this story. This is the last time less'n you want to start sleepin' in the barn."

"Yep, I could feel my old gut blowing up like one of those carnival balloons." He would place his closed hand over his mouth and blow through it like he was blowing up an imaginary balloon, "And then it happened."

Uncle Mooney gave a long pause, and everyone leaned in to hear better, and we all held our breath like it's the first time we've ever heard the story. Just about the time Aunt Mae shifted her position in the rocking chair and started to open her mouth, Uncle Mooney continued. "I grabbed the edge of the top sheet and comforter, sat myself up against the headboard real fast like, pulled those covers up over Mae's head, and just cut loose."

We all shouted, "You didn't!"

"Yeah, I did," Uncle Mooney chuckles, "Made Ebb's barking tree frogs sound like flea whispers. Sounded about like a full-grown elk buglin' during ruttin' time."

"Damn near choked me to death." Aunt Mae glared at him.

"You lived." Uncle Mooney grinned, adding, "I gotta admit though when you came out from under those sheets you were a little green around the gills. And folks," he turned back to the crowd, "she lit into me like a souped-up bobcat. Like to of scratched my eyes out 'fore I could get shut of her."

"And that is why Jimbo was born in December instead of September." Aunt Mae declared with a wag of her finger.

"Yeah," Uncle Mooney always smiled at the end of the story "Some folks call that there move a Dutch Oven. Myself, I call it birth control."

OPENING DAY

Opening day of deer season is not just another day, it is THE DAY. Anyone who claims differently shouldn't be allowed to buy a huntin' license. I believe missing opening day is not only un-redneck, but maybe even un-American. So, when Momma and Aunt Mae grounded me and Jimbo for two weeks the week before opening day, we had us one serious problem. I won't say we didn't deserve to be punished, but I think the consequences should mirror the offence and they had taken it too far.

Not long before the first day of huntin' season, I turned sixteen and could legally drive. Not that I hadn't been driving backroads since I was fourteen, but now I could cruise right down Main Street, so to celebrate we got J.T. to buy us some beer. Jeremiah Tidas, J.T. for short, was just one of our hometown good ole boys who'd graduated high school with no desire what so ever to leave the area. Several years old than us, he delivered supplies for the local lumberyard, and was more than willing to supply the younger generation's alcoholic needs for a minimal retainer, usually a six pack for himself.

We managed to make two trips up and down Main, drinking those cold ones before Jimbo's dumbass tossed an empty can out the window right in front of the police chief. Lucky for us, the chief had graduated from high school with my dad, so instead of hauling us in, he called Pa. That's where the luck ran out though because Pa brought Momma when he came to town to get us.

Pa drove my truck home. Momma drove me and Jimbo to Aunt Mae's house to drop him off. Aunt Mae met us on the front drive and the lecturin' started. What seemed like a century later, after a lot of butt-chewing, it was decided we both would be grounded for two weeks.

"You can't do that," Jimbo moaned out loud what I had been thinking. "What about opening day?"

The look Aunt Mae and Momma gave Jimbo made me glad he'd opened his big mouth before I could. Before Jimbo could react, Aunt Mae's open hand made contact with the back of Jimbo's head. I'm pretty sure they heard the crack two counties over. When Momma jerked her gaze around to me, I already had my head down, eyes on the ground, and was headed for our vehicle. I caught a quick glimpse of Aunt Mae marching Jimbo into the house as we backed out of the driveway. I couldn't hear what she was saying, but her body language told me Jimbo was in for a long evening.

That weekend was one of the longest of my life. By the time I arrived at school Monday morning, I was so tired of Momma's glares and silent treatment, that I was no longer mad at Jimbo for throwing the beer can out the window. I was even a little worried about him when he didn't show up before the bell rang for us to enter the high school building.

After my first hour English class, I caught up to him in the hall and said, "Hey, where were you this mornin'?"

"Mom wouldn't let me ride the bus. She made me wait until she was ready for work and then drove me. I barely made it to class before the tardy bell." He explained, then shook his head and added, "Man, I'm sorry about that beer can stunt. I don't know why I do stupid things like that."

"Forget about it," I smiled. "We got bigger problems. What are we gonna do 'bout opening day?"

"Ain't got no idea," Jimbo shrugged and headed for class.

I figured on it all week and after the last class of the day on Friday, I found Jimbo and told him I had decided I wasn't missing opening day. I *was* going and if he wanted to go, he'd better be out by the road when I came by in the morning. He looked at me like I'd lost my mind, turned, and left the building.

Saturday morning, I woke up well before sunrise and dressed in the dark. Before going to bed, I'd loaded my rifle, coveralls, and a bottle of doe scent in my truck. A quick check to make sure I had my keys, and I started the nerve-racking job of slipping through the house undetected.

As I eased through the kitchen, I noticed the pastries Momma had prepared for the Opening Day Bake Sale the women's church auxiliary group had every year. The auxiliary group always set up outside the main deer check-in station to sell pies, cakes, and cookies, and all the proceeds went to the Children's Church.

The kitchen counter was lined with boxes full of every kind of cookie Momma knew how to bake along with brownies, fudge, and a couple types of homemade holiday candies. She had placed them into sandwich baggies so they could be sold individually. I figured there was no way she'd miss a few brownies and a chocolate chip cookie or two. Momma knew they were my favorite and if she hadn't been so mad at me, she'd would have hollered at me to come sample them last night.

I was glad to see Pa's pickup was already gone when I slipped out the back door. Easing my truck door open, I pulled it into neutral and started pushing it down the drive. At the edge of the gravel, I stepped in and fired it up, but did not turn on the lights. Thankfully the skies were clear and the light from the moon was just enough to make out the centerline if I drove real slow. I left the lights off for a quarter of a mile, and when I switched them on, the light spooked a big eight-point buck, and he ran off into the woods. The adrenaline shot through me like a long pull of Poppa Ebb's shine, and I couldn't wait to get into my tree stand.

When I rounded the curve passing Jimbo's drive, he came up out of the ditch and nearly scared the bejesus out of me. I was cussin' a blue streak when I got the truck pulled over to the side. He opened the door with the shit-eatin' grin he always wears, tossed in a six-pack of Coca-Cola, and crawled in with his rifle.

"Hope you brought something to eat." He said, "Mom spent all last night makin' pies and cakes for the bake sale. Not a damn thang I could lay hand to that she won't miss."

"No worries," I told him, pulling brownies and cookies from

my coat pockets, "Momma made cookies and brownies, and I swiped us some."

Twenty minutes later, we eased off the blacktop and onto two ruts leading off into the woods. A hundred yards in, I pulled to a stop, shut off the lights, and cut the engine. Jimbo and I split the cookies and brownies, and we each downed a soda before stepping out into the dark. In silence we gathered our guns. I raised my hand in a quick wave across the hood of my old Chevy toward Jimbo, and then I started off towards my tree stand.

A hundred yards out, I started spraying doe urine here and there, finishing with a good amount on the tree at the base of my stand. I could just barely see the seat twelve feet above me when I placed my foot on the first wooden rung of the ladder leading up into the tree. Quickly I climbed up, settled onto the seat, positioned my rifle across my knees, and used a penlight to check my wristwatch. It would be a half an hour before the red orange of the rising sun would color the sky just off to my right. I leaned back to wait. There is something about sitting quietly listening to the woods. All the little sounds as if Mother Earth herself is breathing in and out. On opening day, it is not only calming but also exhilarating.

Just as a thin line of color announced dawn's coming, a sound like slow distant thunder before a storm broke the silence of the morning. It was my stomach and seconds later I felt the next spasm start. Somewhere around my spine, brownies and cookies and Coke were in an all-out war, and every so often the battle would roll forward and the roar of cannons could be heard throughout the woods.

After the third abdominal roar, I began to fear the sound would drive away any deer within a mile of my tree. When the fifth one hit, I knew I was in trouble. Deer were the least of my problems. The battle was moving quickly downward. As I gripped my rifle tight and clinched my butt checks together, sweat began to bead up on my forehead. On the next spasm, I started to pray.

What seemed like an eternity later, but in reality, was

probably less than two minutes, the battle let up. Afraid to move, I sat there white knuckling my rifle, my butt cheeks squeezed tight. As the seconds slipped by, I began to think perhaps all would be okay. I loosened my grip, but still unsure, I did not unclench. Just about the time I thought I was out of the woods, from somewhere deep inside I felt the start of the next spasm. Like the eye of a hurricane, the calm before the next storm, I had been suckered into a false sense of security.

I clenched so hard my buttocks themselves began to spasm and I was afraid they were going to cramp. Sweat not only ran down my forehead, but down my neck and back. I began to pray again—this time more earnestly. All thoughts of baggin' a ten-point buck were completely forgotten. I just wanted to be able to safely make it down the ladder in time to pull my coveralls down before the contents of my stomach spewed forth. I focused all my power on the muscles of my sphincter, waited for another break in the battle, and mentally planned the steps I would take to get to the ground.

The break came suddenly. I gave it a slow count of five to make sure there truly was a truce on, and then stood, my butt cheeks still clenched, and slung my rifle over my shoulder by its strap. Turning around I eased onto the wooden ladder and stood momentarily trying to figure out how to step down without unclenching. It was no use, I couldn't step down without relaxing somewhat, so I took a chance and lowered my right foot to the next rung. All went well. Next my left foot, then my right foot—halfway there. One more left foot and with no warning whatsoever, my stomach rolled, and I shit myself.

Now I'm not talking about a little bit came out. It was a full-fledged, no-holds-barred, full-on, four-alarm-fire, everyone out of the building, evacuation of my bowels. As the biggest portion ran through my underwear and down the left leg of my jeans and coveralls, I felt both relief and disgust. And then the smell hit my nostrils and I knew beyond any doubt no self-respecting deer would come within five miles of me or this tree for the next week.

73

By the time I made it to the ground, the acidic nature of the ooze was beginning to burn the skin on the inside of my legs and all I could think about was getting home to a shower. In a straight-legged wobble, I headed back to the truck, hoping Jimbo wouldn't be too long in his stand and planned on having him drive home. At this point I didn't even care about how much trouble I was going to be in for disobeyin' Momma.

As I cleared the tree line headed back to the truck, I spotted Jimbo's head over the side rail. He was sitting in the bed of my truck with his back to the cab and I thought he was sleeping. When I got close enough, he turned his head to me. The grin he usually wore was gone and before I could say anything, he shook his head and said, "Harold, I shit myself."

I didn't know what else to say but, "Me, too."

Now my truck had cloth seats and I knew from the feel that what had started inside my underwear had by now made its way through my jeans and coveralls and would be all over the seat if I sat down in my truck. With Jimbo's help, I gathered up all the sandwich bags from the brownies and cookies and strategically placed them on the seat. Jimbo got back into the bed, and I eased in behind the steering wheel and started for the house. We'd already decided we'd both grab a shower at Jimbo's house and take whatever punishment was coming.

When I pulled into the drive, not only was Aunt Mae waiting, but Momma was there as well. I stepped out of the truck, sandwich baggies stuck to my butt, and Jimbo rolled out over the side of the bed. All I wanted was to get out of my clothes and take a shower. Momma stepped down off the porch, handed me a piece of paper, and headed to her car without a word. I looked at what she'd handed me, it was the empty packaging of that laxative stuff that comes in a box and tastes like chocolate. To this day I'm not sure if she baked it into the cookies, brownies, or both, and I'm still not brave enough to ask.

Aunt Mae made us strip down and hose off outside before she'd let us go inside to take showers. Our clothes were not salvageable, and it took me months to get the smell out of my truck seats. I still think it is un-redneck and un-American to miss Opening Day—that's with one exception. If your Momma grounds you, you get a pass.

Ringin' In The New Year

If Jimbo was an English Bulldog, his best friend Tator Murphy was an English Mastiff. Tator weighed ten pounds three ounces at birth, and his momma just couldn't keep up with his appetite, so she started feeding him watered down mashed potatoes when he was three weeks old, hence the name Tator. The first day of kindergarten, they had to go over to the junior high to get him a chair.

Toad and Frog Williams were twins that lived just down the road from me. They were a year older than Jimbo and Tator but had failed third grade, so they ended up in the same class. I'm pretty sure those were not the names on their birth certificates, but I never heard them called anything else. They were both tall lanky boys with overly long arms and legs. Couple that with weak chins and it was understandable why they received their nicknames.

Put the four of them together and it was a recipe for disaster, so when Jimbo called me on New Year's Day—the year I was fourteen and told me I should come over and play war with them, I should have known something was up. Bored with sitting around the house, I got permission from Momma and rode my brand-new dirt bike over to Jimbo's house. Well, at least the bike was new to me. Actually, it was one Pa had found somewhere and between the two of us we got it running. When I got there, the four of them met me out front. Each of them had a backpack.

"What's goin' on?" I asked as I stepped off my motorbike and kicked the stand down.

"We're gonna hit the woods and play a game of War." Jimbo said, and all four of them laughed.

"What's so funny about that?" I asked.

"Well." Jimbo said and in lieu of an answer unzipped his backpack and showed me the contents.

It was stuffed completely full of Roman candles. For those of you who have never had the opportunity to shoot off these wonderful little fire hazards let me explain. Imagine a thin tube, somewhere between a straw and the cardboard center in paper towels. Tucked neatly inside are pyrotechnic stars wedged between black powder and delay charges. Once lit, the fuse slowly makes its way through the tube shooting one of the explosive stars out the top every couple of seconds until it reaches the bottom. The advice on the side of the packages clearly state that they should be shot out of a bucket or some other safe container and never out of one's hands. I don't know for a fact that the first person who decided to test these instructions was a redneck, but I feel pretty safe puttin' the thought into the 'highly likely' department. When I looked from Jimbo to the others, they all patted their packs and grinned.

I held my hands out to the sides and shrugged. "I don't have any fireworks."

"That's okay," Jimbo grinned, holding up two additional backpacks, "We're gonna split 'em up evenly as soon as Buford gets here."

"Buford Bernard Franklin?" I asked. Like there was another mother on this earth that would tag her son with such a name.

"Yep." Jimbo answered still grinning.

Buford was the smartest guy in my class and would have been the smartest overall if it hadn't been for Janie Thomson, who was not only the best student, but also the prettiest gal in the whole school. My Pa and Buford's Pa had gone to school together, so from time to time when they hunted together, they'd let me and him tag along.

He showed up five minutes later on his motorcycle, parked it next to mine, and we started discussing teams. Jimbo wanted Tator and Buford on his team, but I didn't think that was fair. It took another fifteen minutes and me threatening to leave before he backed off and agreed to let me have Buford. In the end it was me and Burford and Frog, leaving Jimbo, Tator, and Toad as our opponents.

The rules of war are pretty simple. Each team starts at a given spot in the woods. Over the years we have identified five different locations. *The Big Oak*, which was the biggest oak tree in our neck of the woods. *The Crossing* was simply where a path ended at the creek. When the weather was warmer it was also our favorite swimming hole. *The Bee Tree* was an old hollowed out hackberry full of bees and honey. *The Stump* was the farthest spot from Jimbo's house and was just that: an old tree stump. And finally, there was *The Spot*, which got its name because it was the place where we came up with the idea for our war games.

After we decided where each team would start, we agreed on a start time, and headed for our respective spots. Once the time arrived, the war was on, and the team with the last man standing was the winner. The first game was played when I was nine and Jimbo was seven. We had a bunch of friends over that summer and since we didn't have real weapons, we played with green persimmons. If you got hit, you were out. Over the years, we've played with various objects and weapons, including rocks, black walnuts, eggs, bows and arrows with the tips removed, BB guns, and even once with water balloons. Except with the water balloons, the rule has always been no head shots and no crotch shots.

"I call *The Spot*." Jimbo said as soon as the teams were agreed on and the fireworks split up.

"Fine, we'll take *The Bee Tree*," I said, then turned to Buford and Frog, "Come on let's head out."

Before I could step off, the twin I'd spoken to grinned, "I'm not Frog."

As I looked from him to his twin, I realized there might just be a problem. They were both wearing brand spanking new camouflage coats over faded denim jeans which they had stuffed down into their scuffed black combat boots. Once the fireworks started flying, I had no intentions of stopping to ask who was Frog and who was Toad.

"Come on Frog." I motioned to the other twin and started off, shaking my head as I went.

81

When the three of us reached *The Bee Tree*, I checked my watch. We still had five minutes until starting time. Each of us had two lighters and twenty-seven roman candles. I squatted down on one knee and started drawing battle plans in the dirt. Buford dropped down on his haunches to my right and Frog sat down across from us and crossed one leg over the other like we'd been taught to do back in kindergarten.

"Jimbo will send Tator and Toad straight at us down this here path," I made at a line in the dirt, and then I moved over a bit and drew a jagged squiggle, "while he tries to flank us around this ridge. I've seen him do it a hundred times. It's his signature move."

"What you figure we should do?" Frog asked.

In the few minutes left, I outlined the plan and while Buford and Frog got settled into their respective spots, I hightailed it down a game trail I knew, found just the place I was looking for, and curled up alongside an old fallen log. It was hollow and big enough for me to crawl into but the thought of being trapped inside it with Roman candles being shot through the opening made me decide against such foolishness.

Instead, I quickly buried myself in leaves, leaving myself a place to look out, and waited for Jimbo to show. In a matter of minutes, I saw him coming down the trail. Two Roman candles in his right hand and a lighter in his left, he was jogging along in a half crouch heading for the exact spot I'd pointed out to Buford and Frog. When he reached it, he belly-crawled to the top of the ridge and eased himself up just enough to see down the other side of the rise.

From where I lay, I could not see what he was seeing, but if Buford and Frog had done what I told them to, Jimbo would see them lyin' in wait, or at least he would see their legs sticking out from behind the trees. Jimbo's head popped up and then dropped back to the ground. He lay perfectly still and so did I.

After a long, few seconds, he pushed himself up again and took a much longer look, his eyes scanning the terrain below.

Suddenly, I realized he was looking for me and had to smile. Finally, he eased back onto his belly and then quickly rolled onto his back and for a brief instant looked right at me. I thought my cover was blown, but then he seemed to shrug, inhaled deeply, and whistled the long, lonely call of a whippoorwill three times. As he whistled, he twisted the wicks of the fireworks together and as soon as the third whistle escaped his lips, he put fire to 'em, stood, and turned away from me.

I sprang from the leaves, screamed, "RUN", at the top of my lungs, and set to lighting my own Roman candles. As I had instructed, both Buford and Frog screamed "RUN" back at me and began a retreat. Jimbo must have realized I was behind him and not knowing if my fireworks were lit, did not bother to turn around but instead took his chances and dived headfirst over the ridge. The last thing I saw of him was his boot heels just as the first shot left my candle and whizzed through the air.

Roman candle shots blazed over the ridge as I crossed the short distance in a low crouch from my hollow tree to where Jimbo had disappeared. At the edge of the incline, I dropped on to my back, fished two more candles out, and lit them. As soon as their wicks began to hiss, I rolled onto my stomach and chanced a look over the edge.

Sure enough, my plan was working perfectly. Buford and Frog had retreated twenty yards to a second set of trees and were dug in, laying down a steady barrage of colorful red and green shots back my way. Tator and Jimbo were hugged up to the trees my teammates had abandoned and were returning fire. The whole scene reminded me of one of the old war movies Pa like to watch on Saturday mornin's, when he could wrassle the television away from Sissy.

I knew I was out of range but figured I'd give it a try anyway. When the second set of shots left their cardboard tubes, I elevated the fireworks just a little and continued to do so with each shot until finally when the seventh round exploded it was no more than five feet behind and ten feet above Jimbo's head. He threw a look over his shoulders and an unexpected grin spread across his face. The snap of a twig underfoot behind me was all it took for me to realize I had underestimated my cousin.

"I gotcha!" Toad hollered as a flaming green shot past less than three feet from my right ear and exploded in front of me.

I dropped and rolled just as the eighth shot from both my candles discharged. They soared away and detonated; to this day, I could not tell you where they landed because my eyes were fixed on the twin that was advancing rapidly towards me—two candles of his own leveled. Instinctively, I aimed both of mine at him and watched as two beautiful red shots blasted past him on the left and missed him by mere inches. My rolling turn had taken my arms too far for a clean hit. I figured I was a goner.

But the close call had caused Toad to flinch, and his next two shots went into the ground between us. He was so shocked that he dropped one of the candles on the ground and it continued to shoot alternating red and green flashes into the trunk of a tree some twenty feet away. I didn't know how many shots Toad had left but I knew that both of my sticks were down to their last ones. In the same instant that Toad's remaining stick started to hiss—that all too recognizable sound of a dud fizzling—I managed to bring my two next shots back into line with his chest. But before they fired, Toad realized he was out of ammo. He began to back pedal and before I could adjust my aim, both shots exploded out of my Roman candles and went screaming and hissing right into his crotch.

As bad as I felt about the foul, I knew Jimbo well enough to know he would be advancing on me from behind and leaving Tator to cover my team, so I rolled to my feet, leaving Toad to nurse his singed manhood, and sprinted for the nearest tree. I had just managed to get another set of candles lit when sure enough, Jimbo came over the ridge—guns ablazin'. He was expecting me to be out of the game, so he was purposely shooting high as if to shower me in defeat. One look at Toad and he went into a falling roll.

I fired too quickly and both shots passed through the space where Jimbo had been. Like two long fingers, I followed him with my candles. One firing right after the other, each shot missing him by a foot or two. When he came out of the roll, he dived headfirst behind the only cover available... TOAD. My last shots fired, before I realized Jimbo's tactics. Toad took the full impact square between his shoulder blades, and let out a squeal that dang near curled my toenails. Then I saw a small flame appear at the edge of the giant hole the rounds had left in his new camouflage coat.

"He's on fire!" I hollered and started towards him.

Jimbo rolled him over and swatted at his back until the flames went out then he looked up at me and asked, "You hit?"

I did a quick check and said, "No. How 'bout you?"

"Not yet." He answered.

That's when I realized that he was already lighting another wick.

"Wait!!" I squeaked, throwing both hands up, but the look in Jimbo's eyes said he was in it to win it, so as soon as he got the candle lit and he started to level it, I charged right at him. He was expecting me to run away. My forward charge caught him off guard. As I raced past him, I reached out and snatched the Roman candle from his hand. I managed to put the brakes on and stop after ten or fifteen feet. How many shots had been fired I did not know, but I spun around figuring to end it. I brought the business end of my stick to bear on Jimbo just about the time the wick on the candle he'd just lit hit the first cartridge and exploded directly at me.

The shot from my candle stuck Jimbo dead center of his chest and I swear his collided with my bellybutton at the same instant. My next shot hit him a tad lower, and his next shot set the downy filling in the right shoulder of my coat on fire. The next thing I know, me and Jimbo are whacking at ourselves and each other trying to keep our new Christmas coats from going up in flames.

85

About the time, we got ourselves extinguished, Buford, Frog, and Tator came dragging over the ridge and they had fared no better than the three of us. Tator, it seems, had decided to employ a charge-right-at 'em strategy which neither Buford nor Frog were prepared for and somehow all three had taken multiple hits in the melee. Buford had a singed hole in the side of his coat, Frog had one that nearly matched the one in the back of his twin's coat, and the front of Tator's coat was completely riddled with punctures and tears.

As Frog helped Toad back to his feet, I turned to Jimbo and said, "I don't think this was such a good idea."

He looked around our little group and then smiled and said, "Maybe not, but it sure was fun."

But I have to tell you Jimbo's tune changed drastically when we got back to his house. Aunt Mae took one look at us and hollered for Uncle Mooney. By the time my parents got there, everyone else's had already shown up. There was a lot of talk about whoopin's and groundin's, but in the end Pa took all the father's aside and they had a long discussion. When they came back, Pa went over to his truck and took out a big roll of silver duct tape.

All of the mothers fussed and fumed. I even heard Aunt Mae let a couple of cuss words slip, but the fathers just ignored them and slowly, methodically, taped up every hole and tear in our coats. When they were done, we looked like the biggest bunch of misfits you'd never want to lay eyes on.

"You ain't gonna whoop me?" I asked Pa, a bit confused.

With a smile I recognized as his nope-I've-got-a-better-idea-grin, he patted me on the back and said, "No son. None of y'all are going to get a whoopin'. None of y'all are going to get grounded… but every one of you *are* going to wear those coats to school every day until spring. And if any of us catch you out without them on, then you're gonna each get a whoopin' from all of us."

Every one of those dads met every one of us boys' eyes and

none of us kids had any questions about how serious they were. Now you may think we got off lucky, but let me tell you, junior high kids can be brutal, and I can't remember another winter where spring seemed to take as long to get here.

That was the very last time any of us played war. If you had asked us back then why we quit playin', we'd probably have told you that it was because we had outgrown it. But if we'd been bein' completely honest, it was the ribbin's we took from our fellow students and the daily gripin's and nasty looks we all took from our mothers for the next three months. Those were the real reasons that kept us from ever playing again. To this day, I don't much care for Roman candles or silver duct tape.

Me and Jimbo are grown with kids of our own and even now when that New Year's Day is mentioned we shudder. I've heard it said that war is hell and I'm sure it is, but even war can't compare to the wrath of those mothers who didn't get their way. And to be honest, I'd still rather take a whoopin' than have to endure the glare my mother shoots at me every time that particular Christmas coat is brought up.

LOVE STINKS

Now we all know that love is a fickle thing at best, but add it to a Jimbo infatuation, and you've got yourself the recipe for an absolute catastrophe. July in our part of the world was known for breaking record temperatures, and this here summer the weather decided to set a new record just about every other day. Let's just say that if hell is any hotter than that July was, then it's sure not where I want to spend my eternity.

Our town, like most, had a local group, mostly made up of volunteer firefighters, who put on a fireworks display on the fourth. The only reason for not going was because you had a girlfriend in another town and was attending hers, which in my case was not a problem. And as it happened, Jimbo was also unattached, so we piled into my old truck, had J.T. buy us two six-packs of beer and headed for the show.

I don't know how they set things up in your town, but in ours, there was a big field beyond the south end of the high school football stadium. A good portion of it was plowed under and the fire department assembled there with their engines and the year's pyrotechnics. Both home and visitor's bleachers were available for seating during the festivities, but the adults and good students mostly used the home stands, and those with questionable morals and ethics were more likely to be found in or behind the visitors.

A large asphalt-paved lot south of the high school itself served for parking. It was also the reason our school and some of the students had begun to act a bit more highfalutin'. Ours was one of the first schools in the area to get a blacktop. It always amazed me how a little petroleum mixed with rock could make some folks so snobbish.

Between the school and the football stadium, vendors were allowed to set up and hawk their wares. For five to ten dollars, the powers that be would sell you a space. The price differential was supposed to keep the junk swappers and dog traders separated from the more serious arts and crafts people. It wasn't always this way. At one time all of the areas were the same size and priced at two and a half dollars.

Then one year old Ned Duke brought a litter of half-grown bluetick hounds to sell. That was not an uncommon occurrence, since many of the local hunters used the event as a means of making a little extra money. The problem occurred when he got to visiting with a couple of other breeders about whose dogs were better at treeing and one of those pups decided the wildlife in Ida Mae Gibson's canvas paintings was too realistic. First, they began to bay. Old Ned used the noise as proof his dogs were born ready to go huntin', and never bothered to check and see what had them riled up. Ida Mae was bickering with a potential client on the other side of her space when the whelp in question got loose and completely demolished two of her paintings. By the time Mr. Duke got him under control, he had gnawed the squirrel out of one canvas and had set to removing a raccoon's head from another.

After the incident the other breeders said it was proof that Old Ned's dogs were inferior, claiming any dog that tried to tree such a poor depiction of wildlife had something wrong with it. Ida Mae was absolutely livid at the destruction of the hard work she had put into her craft and became even more so when she heard the critique of her artistic abilities. I can't say as I know what the outcome of the whole debacle was, or if Mr. Duke had to make restitution or not but by the time the next year rolled around, the vendor prices had been raised and a new arrangement of spacing had been put in place.

When we got to the field, I parked behind the visitor's stands next to Buford's old green Buick. He and Tator were kicked back against the hood watching the girls as they passed by and arguing about which ones they could get if they had the desire to try.

"Y'all ready to go check it out?" Jimbo hollered as he crawled out the window of my truck. The latch in the passenger door had busted the week before, and I hadn't got around to fixing it. I was just happy the window still rolled up and down.

"What about Frog and Toad?" Tator hollered back.

"You snooze, you lose." Jimbo laughed, "They'll catch up. Let's go see what's cookin'."

With that the four of us ambled around the field towards the market booths. As we walked, Tator looked over at Jimbo and said, "Heard you was a free man, again."

"Yep." Jimbo nodded, "Lori's family's movin' somewhere down in Texas, and you know me, I just ain't no good at long-distance relationships."

Buford laughed, "Hell, Jimbo you ain't good at any type of relationship less'n it's a short-term affair."

Jimbo feigned indignation and said, "Now that ain't true. Me and Lori was about to have our two-month anniversary."

Buford shook his head, "You're right..." Buford frowned, "... for you that's damn close to a life sentence."

"You know," I interrupted, "I think I want to find someone who I really like, someone who I want to spend the rest of my life with before things get too serious."

"Yeah, right," Jimbo guffawed, "You're just scared if you get too serious, you'll get some girl pregnant, and your momma'll skin ya."

Buford came to my defense, "I don't know, I think maybe Harold has a point. Maybe we should be listenin' to our hearts more. Like the heart should be our compass."

"Don't know about y'all," Jimbo grinned, "But if my heart is my compass, then my pecker is the needle."

I just looked over at Buford and we both shook our heads. Jimbo and Tator broke into a laughing spell that continued until we made it to the first set of vendors.

We strolled along checking out the wares, until we reached the fourth stall. It had a little table set up with three metal cages

93

on it. The first cage had Siamese kittens for sale, the second a single Chihuahua puppy, and the third had four baby skunks. Now this wasn't the first time I'd seen these little striped rodents at the event, but it was the first time I'd ever seen Janie Thomson showing an interest in anything but her studies and band.

I'd had a crush on Janie since the third grade but no one but Pa knew it and thank goodness he wasn't the kind to spill the beans. Anyway, there she was with Becca Jones, both of them holding little baby skunks and just chatting away with the merchant.

"Why don't they stink?" Becca was asking.

"Because they've had their scent glands removed," the lady selling the skunks told her.

"Oh, I see," Becca turned and looked at Janie, "I sure would like to have one."

"Can you afford it?" Janie asked Becca, and handed hers back to the vendor.

"No." Janie answered and handed her black and white baby back to the lady as well. "I spent all my money on clothes and a few fireworks."

As the lady put them back into their cage, she said, "If you change your mind, I'll be here 'til it's over."

The four of us had walked up and were standing behind them. Not realizing we were there, when Janie turned to leave, she ran square into me, and we both began to stammer apologizes. Where I found the courage, I will never know, maybe it was the July heat frying the gray matter in my head, or the way the floral scent of her Fabergé Babe perfume filled the air around us, but in a momentary stupor I said, "Would you like to sit with me for the fireworks show?"

She reached out, took my hand, and said, "I thought you'd never ask." And that began a long and wonderful relationship, but that's a story for another time.

Jimbo was never one to let me have too much glory, so as soon as Janie agreed to sit with me, he, with a grand flourish, bowed at the waist, looked up at Becca, and said, "And you my dear Becca, would you kindly allow me to accompany you this evening?"

"I reckon not." She answered.

That girl might as well have struck him across the face with a glove and challenged him to a duel because rejection was just a game of chess played with checkers to Jimbo, and the game was on.

For the next two weeks Jimbo was relentless. He called Becca every day until her mother threatened to call Aunt Mae if he did not stop phoning their house. Then he began to make regular stops at the Burger Shop where Becca worked. That's not to say that some of those stops weren't necessary for a meal or a drink, but he was there so often they probably should have put him on the payroll. Still, she would not budge, and made it clear that she wanted nothing to do with Jimbo.

Along about the middle of the month, Jimbo called and asked if I wanted to go fishing. I had been spending quite a bit of time with Janie and didn't really want to, but his whining got the best of me. I knew he was feeling down and figured he needed some company. When I found out he had invited the whole crew, and my presence wasn't really all that necessary, I was a little peeved.

Tator had brought along some beer and the twins had swiped a half full bottle of their dad's Wild Turkey. Jimbo loaded up with me while the other four followed behind us in Buford's Buick. As soon as we cleared town, Jimbo cracked open his first beer and by the time we got to our fishing hole, he had finished off his second and all he wanted to talk about was Becca.

An hour and another two beers into the trip, and he was still whining and carrying on about how he could not figure out why she wouldn't at least give him a chance. "Maybe it's because she's a senior this year and you're an underclassman." Buford offered.

"Ain't no law against her datin' a junior." Jimbo declared and popped open yet another brewski.

"No, there ain't no law against it but name me one senior girl you ever knew who dated anyone in a lower grade." Buford countered.

Jimbo fiddled with his pole for a minute unable to come up with anyone. Tator, who always loved name-me-one-person games, jumped up off the log he was sitting on, pointed at Buford, and said, "Beverly Hogg, she dated a junior her senior year."

"Who the hell is Beverly Hogg?" I asked, "You makin' this up?"

"No." Tator pouted, "She's my second cousin, or maybe my third."

"When did she graduate?" Buford asked.

"Seven or eight years ago." Tator poked out his chest in victory.

"Ain't nobody named Hogg graduated from our school." I shook my head and looked up at him.

"Never said she was from our school," Tator proclaimed, "She graduated out at…"

"That don't count." Buford cut him off.

"Why not?" Tator whined.

"Because it don't, that's why." I said, "It has to be someone from our school."

"Buford never said that." Tator bellyached and sat back down.

By the time Jimbo and Tator finished off the beer, Toad and Frog had emptied the whiskey bottle, and since none of us had even got one bite, we decided to call it a day. We loaded our rods and the old Igloo cooler Jimbo had brought into the bed of my truck and started back towards town with Buford leading the way. Halfway back, Jimbo started whining that he needed to pee.

"Can't ya hold it 'til we get to your house?" I asked.

"Don't think so." He answered, so I pulled over and he crawled out the window I still hadn't fixed.

Just as he finished his business and got his pants zipped up, a momma skunk followed by five little babies walked out of the woods not fifty yards up the road. One of them must have stepped on a twig because all of a sudden Jimbo's head snapped around in their direction and before I could blink, he was off at a dead run. That mama skunk must have heard him coming because she scampered across the road and into the underbrush like a shot with her babies pushing hard to keep up. By the time Jimbo caught up to them he had peeled his shirt off, and as the last little one cleared the road, he launched it like a fishing net. As luck would have it, Jimbo's aim was true, and the final little skunk must have thought the sky had fallin' on him because it just froze. That was all the time Jimbo needed. He bent down and wrapped that baby up in his shirt and was just about to stand up with it, when that old momma decided to let loose. Jimbo took the full force of her fury in his face and chest.

I threw my truck door open and started to crawl out. I thought first only of Jimbo's safety but as soon as the smell hit me, my thoughts turned to Janie and I, knowing how long that smell would last if it got on me, I quickly back tracked and stood in front of the truck.

Jimbo dropped to all fours and scooted backwards across the asphalt on his hands and knees. Standing by my truck, I could hear him choking and gagging. About the time he made it into the grass on the opposite side of the road, he began to puke and all that beer he'd been drinking spewed out of him in a steady stream. Somewhere between the vomiting and the dry heaving, he started wiping his face across one of his arms. That baby skunk was still rolled up in his shirt squirmin' and squealin'. Jimbo, blind as he was, held on to that shirt like his life depended on it.

When he finally found his wind, he shouted, "Harold... Harold, help me man, I'm blind."

I stood there feeling bad clean to the center of my core, but every time I started to move forward, my brain would once again begin to calculate how long it would be before Janie would let me set next to her if I got that stink on me. "Can't do it." I hollered at him.

"Oh, come on, man," he whined, and I thought for sure that he was gonna start cryin', "I'd do it for you."

I knew that was an outright lie, and somehow that in itself made me feel better about not advancing. "Can you stand up?" I bellowed.

"I think so," he answered, "but I cain't see shit."

"That's okay," I reassured him, "just stand up and follow my voice."

A bit shaky he stood to his feet and slowly started my way. I eased back and took up a new position behind my truck door. When I was sure he was headed in the right direction, I crawled over and rolled up the passenger side window. By the time I stepped back out, he had almost made it to the front of the truck.

"Five more steps and you're at the truck," I guided him in, "put your hands out, one more step."

His right hand touched the housing of the headlight and he began to work his way down the side of the truck. When he reached the door and found the window up, he began to howl, "Come on Harold, let me in."

"Ain't gonna happen." I shouted back at him. "Crawl up in the back… And let that baby skunk loose."

After several minutes of arguing, he finally gave up on the idea he was going to ride home in the cab but refused to let the little one go. He kept saying it was the answer to all his problems. At the time that made no sense at all to me.

I'm pretty sure folks could smell us coming from at least a quarter of a mile away and by the time I pulled into Aunt Mae and Uncle Mooney's driveway the smell had already seeped into the front with me. At some point during the trip, Jimbo had managed to get the skunk out of his shirt and into the empty cooler and was wiping at himself with his shirt when I parked.

I don't know if it was the smell that brought Aunt Mae out of the house, but as soon as she cleared the door, she shouted over her shoulder at Uncle Mooney. I skirted the truck, avoiding Jimbo, and began to explain the events that had led to Jimbo's current predicament, leaving out the alcohol, of course. Jimbo still could not see but had managed to get himself out of the truck and using our voices started to move towards us. I began to fear I was going to upchuck myself. In self-defense, the three of us began to move away.

When Aunt Mae had had enough, she shrieked, "Jimbo, you stop right there!!!"

Jimbo froze in his tracks and then just sat down right there in the middle of the yard.

"Mooney, you get the garden hose and start spraying him off while I go get the tomato sauce," Aunt Mae said.

Uncle Mooney started around the side of the house and Aunt Mae ordered Jimbo to strip before disappearing into the house herself.

I had no desire to see Jimbo in his boxers or to watch the scrubbing that was about to commence, so I hollered through the stink to where Jimbo was sitting, "See ya later, cuz."

He raised a hand, then as I started away, hollered, "Hey, Harold, can you get the baby skunk out of the cooler and put it in the old rabbit hutch out back?"

"I guess so," I said, "you sure you don't want me to just let it loose."

"Hell no," he shouted, "I'm gonna tame it down and give it to Becca. She's sure to fall in love with me then."

Looking back, I reckon I should have lied and told him it got loose when I tried to move it from the cooler into the hutch, but at the time it seemed harmless, so I did as he asked. And to his credit, he did spend the next five weeks taming that little fella down. Two days before the first day of school, he found an old boot box and poked a couple of holes in one of its sides. Then he cut up some brown grocery sacks from the Piggly Wiggly and wrapped it up nice, even found some left over Christmas ribbon in one of Aunt Mae's closets and put a big old red bow on the top.

I figure Cupid, that's what he named the skunk because he said it was the arrow that was gonna win him Becca's love, was about four months old by the time Jimbo got it good and tamed. And I have to admit, he was a cute little fella. He would even take pieces of dry cat food right out of your fingers.

When Jimbo finally got the box together just the way he wanted it, he called me and asked if I would run him down to the Burger Shop. Of course, I wanted to know why, and he explained that Aunt Mae wouldn't allow him to borrow the car if he was going to be transporting "that damn rodent", her words not mine.

"Where're ya takin' Pepé Le Pew?" Uncle Mooney asked, he refused to call the skunk Cupid.

"To Becca." Jimbo answered.

"Ain't a good idea." Uncle Mooney said.

"How so?" Jimbo asked.

"Pepé there still has his equipment and he's 'bout old enough to start usin' it." Uncle Mooney told him.

"I tamed him down good." Jimbo said, "He ain't gonna spray no one."

"You better hope not." Uncle Mooney said, "Better let Becca know he ain't been fixed just to be on the safe side."

"I will." Jimbo assured him.

And with that we were off to the Burger Shop. Since this was Jimbo's bailiwick, when we got there, I found a booth way clear to the rear of the dining area near the back door and slid into it. Jimbo waltzed right up to the counter and asked Becca if she would come sit with him for a minute. From my spot, I could not hear the words, but the attitude was a definite no. Then to my surprise, Jimbo held up that wrapped box and began to walk away and Becca just followed right along like a little pup after a ham bone.

Next thing I know they're sittin' at a table, and she is unwrapping that box, paper just a flying. When she got the paper off and the lid open, she took one look into Cupid's cute little face and let out a squeal of pure joy. And for just a split second, I believe Jimbo had truly won her heart. But that squeal caught Cupid off guard and in a flash, he spun around, tail up. I guess

Jimbo suspected what was coming next, because he tried to slam the lid of that box back shut, but he just wasn't quick enough. A pungent fog of toxic musk escaped out of the cracks and formed a cloud around their table.

In one quick motion, I slid from my booth and right out the back door. I did not even think twice about it, nor did I for one single second feel bad about it. I knew all hell was about to break loose, and I wanted no part of it. I went straight to my truck, rolled up both windows, and locked the doors. I was sitting there waiting, five minutes later when Jimbo came out carrying Cupid in his box. Once again, he and Cupid rode home in the bed of my truck, and once again Jimbo got to strip down to his skivvies and endure a scrubbing.

Aunt Mae put her foot down, and said that Cupid was going to the woods, and if Jimbo wanted to keep him, then he could go with him. For a few years after that I always wondered if it was Cupid when I would see a skunk out and about. Jimbo and Becca never did get together. As a matter of fact, I do not think Becca ever spoke to him again. They both showed up on the first day of classes still smelling strongly of skunk, and I can't say I blame Becca for her feelings towards Jimbo. That, by all accounts, was an extremely terrible way to begin your senior year of high school.

Along about the end of the first nine weeks of school, Jimbo asked me one evening, "So how long you figure you and Janie are gonna last?"

"I can't say for certain yet," I told him, "but this could be the one. I think she loves me, and I know I'm in love. How 'bout you, you got anyone in your scopes?"

"Oh, hell no," he said, "I learned my lesson this summer. As far as I'm concerned, love stinks, and it's just better if I play the field."

In Jimbo's case, I had to agree.

In addition to this collection of short stories, this author also has the following full length novel available:

The first two chapters of *The Road to Nowhere* have been included in the following pages for you.

THE
ROAD
TO
NOWHERE

CHARLES LEMAR BROWN

CHAPTER 1

Will Tucker was a cantankerous old bastard. Fifty years of ranching in the heart of Oklahoma had left him iron hard and leather tough. He had earned every wrinkle on his clean-shaven weathered face. Years of riding fence aboard an old hammerhead roan had left him slightly bow-legged, and the hours spent perched on his old John Deere tractor had given him a permanent squint. Deep-set hazel eyes, a saturnine nose, and silver hair gave him an almost aristocratic appearance—at least until he opened his mouth. He rarely spoke, but when he did, the deep gravelly Okie twang in his voice got the attention of everyone around. At five ten and a hundred and eighty-five pounds, he was seldom the biggest or tallest man in the room, but he had a way of making everyone he met feel like they were looking up at him.

Today Will rode his favorite mount, a big red roan quarter horse. Together, they plodded methodically north toward a tree line a half mile away. At fifteen and a half hands, the quarter horse was an animal that turned heads. On a normal day, the gelding would be pulling hard, wanting to run, but he could sense the frustration in his rider and so held back.

The problem, as Will had labeled his current dilemma, was not one that could be taken care of with a simple ride around the family's vast cattle ranch. It was not the kind a little duct tape and bailing wire could fix, and that was what had Will's mind in turmoil. He liked life simple.

"Red, I'm pissed." Will finally spoke to his horse.

Red pulled against the reins and then relaxed. Will smiled at the simplicity of the horse's action. With one simple gesture, the horse had said you are still the boss, but I am ready whenever you are. All you have to do is give the signal. He and the horse had been together a long time, and sometimes Will thought the dang animal knew him better than any human, maybe better than he even knew himself.

"Okay, then old boy, let'er fly." he said with a clicking sound and leaned forward to get Red moving.

Red sprang forward into full gallop. The horse and rider moved as one. A quarter of a mile, a half mile, the land blurred past. Another quarter of a mile and the tree line loomed large. Will eased him back to a canter as they passed through the trees and into a clearing lined with scrub oaks and mountain cedars. They crossed the clearing at a trot and Will reined him back to a walk as he found the head of a cattle trail leading off to the northwest.

A half mile further and Will pulled up at the edge of a pond. Several red-eared turtles perched on a snag at the water's edge surveyed the newcomers warily. When Will dismounted, the largest of them slid quickly into the safety of the water. He removed his old worn sweat-stained straw Stetson hat and slapped it against the thigh of his faded, creased Wranglers to remove dust. The remaining turtles disappeared.

Red stood front feet in the water and drank. Will stared silently out across the land. He loved this ranch. He could smell dirt from a freshly plowed field, see a small bunch of his Hereford cattle off to the west, and hear the call of a western meadowlark searching for company. How anyone could not love this land was beyond his comprehension. The few years he had been away during the war, all he could think about was getting back. Once back, he had refused to leave, and for over fifty years, there had been no reason to do so. Now the time had come, and he did not like it—not one little bit.

Will took a canteen down from the horn of his saddle, unscrewed the cap, and drank. Recapping the canteen, he wiped his mouth on the sleeve of his blue denim, pearl-snapped

Wrangler work shirt. A calf bawled, and Red's head snapped up—ears back, eyes searching. Will rubbed the horse's neck, replaced the canteen, gathered the reins, and mounted.

The north fence was still a mile away, and he wanted to check it before supper. As he rode, his eyes studied the land. Not in an obvious way, but in the more natural way of an animal accustomed to its place in the world. He had ridden over every inch of this land, both with his father and with his grandfather, so many times that he knew it as well as he knew his own face. Each had taught him much.

He had tried to do his part. He had added acres to the land he had inherited. He had done his best to pass on the love of the land to his sons and his grandson. Perhaps if Wyatt had lived, it would have been different. Wyatt had truly loved the ranch. Will had never doubted the future of the Rolling T when Wyatt was alive. The small family cemetery near the ranch's northwest corner came into view. Frustrated, Will shook his head.

At the entry to the cemetery, Will pulled Red to a stop and looked over the split-wood rail fence that surrounded the graves. His grandparents, his parents, his only brother, his daughter-in-law, and Wyatt all rested within. He remembered too well the day they had gotten the call. Wyatt had been in an accident. An eyewitness said he had swerved to avoid a head-on collision with a red vehicle. Wyatt had lost control and slammed head on into a tree. The red car had never even slowed down, the driver was never found. Their little family had not been the same since. Bo, Wyatt's older brother, had slowly drifted away from ranching and towards other interests. Will knew it was because the ranch held to many memories of his brother. It was not that Bo did not do his share of the work or help keep the ranch going, it was simply that Will could tell his heart was not really in it.

Will's eyes drifted to his brother Fred's grave. On two different occasions during the war, his brother had saved him from death. He had personally seen Fred do the same for at least three other soldiers. Will himself had been awarded a silver star for a charge he made that enabled a group of injured soldiers to be rescued. What the official record of the heroic deed failed to mention was that Will had thought Fred was among those pinned down by enemy fire. It was not until after everyone was safe that Will would find out his brother's orders had been changed and he was elsewhere, leaving Will to wonder if he had known Fred was not there, would his actions have been different.

The two of them had always been close. They had grown up riding this very land, but the war and the atrocities they had seen there had given them a bond not many would understand. It had also given them the one thing they could never agree on — who really deserved the silver star.

With a click of his tongue Will started Red forward once again. At the northwest corner post, he turned and started east. As he rode, he watched for slack in the barbed wire, wooden posts that would need to be replaced soon, and tracks of any animals that might have passed this way. This was all part of his normal Saturday afternoon routine and usually one of his favorite times of the week. The problems and frustrations of the past several days typically faded away as he rode, but the events of the previous week continued to wear on him. He shifted in the saddle, made a mental note that the corner post at the east end of the fence line was looking a little weathered, and then he turned the horse to the south. He and Bo had replaced the old wooden fence posts here with new T-post last summer. Using the metal post was the smart thing to do, he knew, but he sure missed the look of the old weathered wooden ones.

The sun was easing towards the western horizon by the time he had gotten back to the barn. He curried Red and turned him out. The red, step-side Chevy pickup parked in the gravel beside the western-style, cedar-sided ranch house told him Bo was over for a late supper. Fried chicken, mashed potatoes and gravy, and homemade rolls usually sounded good after an afternoon of riding, but Will just couldn't seem to find his appetite.

110

*****

Margaret Tucker watched out the kitchen window as her husband curried Red and turn him out. Something was eating at Will, but she was no fool. If she asked him about it, he would just grunt and wave a hand in denial, so she would wait. She was good at waiting. When you live in the middle of nowhere, you had better be. She was a kind, patient, and very caring woman. At five foot eight, she was almost as tall as her husband. At one hundred and twenty pounds she moved with the grace of a model. Dying her hair would have made her look half her age, but she chose not to dye it. It was sprinkled with just enough gray to give her a regal appearance, and she usually wore it in a bun on top of her head.

She removed her white kitchen apron and hung it in its place on the back of the pantry door. Smoothing the front of her blue calico dress with her hands, she stepped back and surveyed the solid oak table that sat eight. It was topped with a red and white checkered tablecloth. Three places were set, each with a solid white Corelle plate, knife and spoon to the right, and a fork atop a white cloth napkin to the left. Above and to the right of each place setting was a quart mason jar half filled with ice. A platter of fried chicken was placed near one end of the table and around it were bowls of mashed potatoes, gravy, corn on the cob, and homemade rolls.

"Smells good, Maggie," Will called half-heartedly from the mud room.

"Thanks," Maggie replied, "It's ready when you are."

"Be right there." Will knocked the dust from his clothes and boots and washed his hands in the wall hung sink next to the back door.

Maggie placed a pitcher of sweet tea on the table as Will stepped through the door. Fifty years of marriage at the end of the month and she still got butterflies when he walked into a room and smiled at her. She straightened her dress once again, stepped around the table, and kissed him on the cheek.

"How was your ride?" she asked.

111

"Fine," Will answered, then added, "Fences looked good."

Bo came in from the living room. A younger version of Will, he was an inch taller and ten-pounds lighter. A shiny, slick-shaven head kept the grey from showing, but it did nothing for the streaks that shot through his mustache and goatee. Once he had worn a smile that was contagious, now he seldom smiled at all.

"Looks delicious, mom," he stated flatly as he pulled out a chair and slid into it.

Will took his place at the head of the table, and Maggie sat down beside him, across from Bo, who stretched his arm across the table and took his mother's hand as Will took the hands of his wife and son. Together, they bowed their heads.

Will prayed, "Heavenly Father, thank You for this day. Thank You for this family. Thank You for this food. Please bless it to the nourishment of our bodies. We ask it all in Jesus' name. Amen."

Maggie gave each of the men's hands a little squeeze before she released them. Will reached for the fried chicken, and Bo grabbed the bowl of mashed potatoes. Bowls and platters where shuffled until all three had full plates. Will worked on a corn cob briefly then set it at the back of his plate.

"Did last night's supper bother anyone else?" he asked as he picked up his fork then set it back down again.

Last night had bothered Maggie, but how to put her feelings into words just wouldn't come, so she kept her peace. She was glad, on one hand, that Will had opened the conversation and that she knew now what had been eating at him all day, but on the other hand, she was at a loss as how to further the conversation. Bo swallowed a mouth full of chicken and wiped his mouth.

"Yep, Pa," he answered, then added, "The whole situation plum pisses me off, 'scuse the French Momma, but it does."

"Have you talked to that boy?" Will asked staring hard at Bo.

That boy was William Mark Tucker. Trey to his family because he was the third William in line and Bo's only child, Will and Maggie's only grandchild. Four years ago, he had been valedictorian of his senior class and a pretty good high school baseball pitcher. Murray State College in Tishomingo, Oklahoma, had recruited him to pitch for the Aggies, but he had turned that down and accepted a full ride academic scholarship to East Central University in Ada, Oklahoma, so he could be with his high school sweetheart. On the previous day, Trey and Lisa, now his fiancé, had graduated from the university and had been treated by Will to supper at Santa Fe Steakhouse in Ada.

"Yep." Bo stared hard back, "I've talked 'til I'm blue in the face, but he ain't listenin'. He's smitten."

"When's he comin' home?" Will asked.

"Supposed to be in late tonight," Bo answered around another bite of chicken, swallowed then continued, "He's gonna drop Lisa off with her friends up at Will Rogers airport before he comes in. Why?"

"You're not eatin', darlin'," Maggie said glancing over at Will.

"Give me a minute," Will responded and stared aimlessly at his plate.

"Pa, you got something on your mind?" Bo wiped his mouth, laid his napkin down, and sat waiting.

After a long minute, Will spoke, "My grand pappy use to say, 'Son, when you have a problem, you mull it over good, figure a way to fix it, then get to fixin'.'" He twisted his mouth sideways, thought a minute more, then added, "I been thinkin' 'bout this problem all day long, and I think it's time to get to fixin'."

"And just how do you plan to do that?" Maggie asked.

Will smiled and raised an eyebrow.

Bo grinned, "I've seen that look before. What have you got up your sleeve?"

"Okay, but first, did either of you notice Trey's reaction when that cute little waitress asked him if they'd been in Calculus II together?" Will asked.

"Yeah," Bo nodded his head, "He looked like he wanted to swallow his spoon and crawl under the table."

"And his fiancé looked like she could have driven her steak knife into the waitress and not even thought twice about it." Will added.

"I felt bad for her." Maggie said.

"For who? The waitress or Trey's fiancé?" Will asked.

"The waitress," Maggie answered, then, "She seemed like such a sweet child. She sure didn't deserve the way Lisa treated her or Trey for that matter."

"Yes, and if I had to guess, Trey caught hell all night long and maybe all day long too." Bo reddened.

"Yep." Will nodded and picked up his fork.

Maggie and Bo watched as he loaded it with mashed potatoes and gravy and took a bite. He chewed, swallowed, cut a piece from his chicken breast, and placed it in his mouth. Bo, not knowing what else to do, picked up his fork and began to eat. Maggie waited patiently until each had taken several bites.

"Do you have a plan or not." She shook her head as she asked the question.

"Course I do," Will answered around another fork of mashed potatoes.

"Care to share?" Bo queried as he pulled a hot roll apart.

Will swallowed, placed his fork so that it rested on the right side of his plate, wiped his mouth, took a long swig of sweet tea, then slowly nodded.

Bo stopped eating, took a drink of tea, and wiped his mouth. Maggie pursed her lips and drew her eyebrows down hard.

"Okay, okay," Will held up a hand, "Don't get you're…"

"Don't finish that sentence." Maggie cautioned, lowering her head and raising her eyebrows.

Will held up the other hand and leaned back laughing, then asked, "Maggie is your great-niece still getting married out in California?"

"I'll play along," Maggie answered, "Yes she is, why?"

"Didn't you say we got an invite in the mail?" Will returned.

"Oh, so you were listening?" Maggie replied.

"I'm always listening," Will stated.

Bo chuckled.

"What's so damn funny?" Will snapped.

"You two act like an old married couple." Bo laughed again.

"How dare you call your momma old." Will feigned shock.

"Enough," Maggie nearly shouted.

Will enjoyed the banter, but he knew when he'd pushed far enough. Now that he had the attention of both of them and knew they had similar thoughts about the situation, it was time to lay out his plan.

"I think what Trey needs is some time away," he said, "time away from that fiancé, time away from Caddo County, time away from Oklahoma. I think it's time for a little trip."

"Okay, I'll agree," Bo chimed in.

"Me, too," Marge agreed.

"Bo can't leave because he's got summer baseball," Will reminded them.

"I don't think he'll go by himself," Maggie said, "He really doesn't know those folks out there that well. As a matter of fact, except for my sister Amelia, none of us do."

"Don't worry," Will said with a nod, "He'll be driving us."

"Us?" Maggie looked puzzled, "Us, like you and I?"

"Yep." Will smiled.

"Pa, when was the last time you left Oklahoma?" Bo's voice registered shock.

"Two years before you were born," Maggie answered, then to Will, "You sure about this?"

"Bad as I hate travelin', I hate what that girl is doin' to our grandson even more," Will nodded his head in affirmation, "She's changed since they went off to college and what's more Trey has allowed her to change him. It's time to get to fixin' the problem, and it looks to me like we're gonna have to do it since he seems to have his head too far up… well, y'all get the picture. Bo, do you think you can get Bud Wilkerson to help you with the ranch while we're gone?"

"I think so, but how are you gonna convince Trey to go?" Bo asked.

"Ain't gonna be no convincing. He got a full scholarship, but not a meal ticket. The deal was I paid his meal ticket, and he worked it off during the summer. He still owes me a summer of work," Will answered.

"Yes, but that was ranch work, pa," Bo said.

"Never stipulated what kind of work," Will grinned mischievously. "Looks like this summer he's a chauffeur."

Maggie shook her head. "That's not funny, Will."

"Sure, it is," Will shot back.

"When do you want to leave?" Maggie asked.

"After church tomorrow good with you?" Will asked in return.

"Lordy, Will, you got to give a lady time to pack," Maggie fussed. "How 'bout first thing Monday morning."

"Alright, then," Will nodded towards Bo's plate. "Your dinner's gettin' cold, better eat up."

Bo laughed, picked up his fork, filled it with mashed potatoes, and began the process of cleaning his plate. Maggie shook her head in disbelief, and the three continued with their supper, feeling better now that there was a plan for fixin' the problem.

Lord, help Trey, Maggie thought to herself and wondered if her son and husband were thinking the same thing.

CHAPTER 2

Trey eased his red Nissan Altima into a space on the south end of the church in Fort Cobb. The building was a single-story, light brown brick structure with dark brown shingles and a wooden sign out front identifying the property as the First Baptist Church. A silver sedan pulled through the circle driveway and dropped off an elderly lady at the front entrance, then pulled around to the additional parking on the north side of the building.

Two spaces down from where Trey had snagged a parking place, he noticed a dark blue F150. A gray-haired man in a western suit got out, circled the vehicle, and opened the door for his wife. The two of them walked hand in hand towards the front entrance. Trey wondered if they had always held hands or if it was something that came with age. He and Lisa seldom held hands. His eyes strayed from the couple back to the truck they had exited. He wasn't a Ford man himself, but it was a nice truck. He sure missed his old Silverado, but Lisa thought the Altima said 'accountant' more than a big Chevy pickup.

He opened the door, slid out of the vehicle, straightened his pressed white western shirt, adjusted his belt buckle, and started for the front door of the church. His dark-brown, pleated, Wrangler Riata dress pants stacked up just right over his tan, square-toed ostrich boots. Inside the church, he weaved a path through the folks congregated in the foyer visiting between Sunday school and the morning service and found his way to the men's room. In the mirror, he did a quick check of his hair and then straightened his western print necktie. Staring at his reflection, he suddenly realized how much he looked like the picture of his dad that sat on the hutch in Granny and Pappy's living room. His hair was longer, and he combed it over to the right instead of straight back the way his dad had in his younger years, but the resemblance was uncanny.

Leaving the restroom, Trey found the foyer empty except for a small boy who was stretched on tiptoes trying to get a drink out of the aluminum water fountain. Trey remembered when he had trouble with the very same fountain, crossed to the child, and hoisted him up long enough to get a drink.

"Thanks mister." The boy ran off laughing into the sanctuary.

Mister? That seemed a little odd. Mister was his dad or his granddad. He wasn't old enough to be a mister yet. *To the boy I'm a mister, to my dad and grandad I'm still a snot-nosed kid. Interesting,* Trey thought, *I guess not everything you learn comes from college and books. I guess, age is definitely relative.*

Folks were milling around visiting, hugging, and shaking hands when Trey entered the sanctuary. A dozen men shook his hand, and several older ladies grabbed him for a hug as he made his way down the center aisle towards his family's pew. Officially, there were no assigned pews, unofficially, you could look forward to dirty looks, hateful attitudes, and a whole lot of unChristian-like spirits if you sat in the wrong pew. It was just better to sit where you were supposed to rather than to tempt the Fates.

Trey slid in beside his grandmother. She leaned over and gave him a hug just as the youth pastor stepped up to the pulpit and asked the congregation to bow their heads so he could lead them in prayer. When he finished, he made a few announcements and then turned the service over to the choir director.

A short, wide man in brown corduroy pants and a red polo shirt rose from a bench and approached the pulpit, and the youth pastor stepped aside. Under his direction the congregation sang "Holy, Holy, Holy" and then "How Great Thou Art". At the end of the second selection, he announced that the twelve-member choir would sing 'All Hail the Power of Jesus Name". As the choir sang, Trey glanced past his grandmother at his grandfather. Will Tucker sat straight in the pew, head and eyes forward, watching the choir sing. On the other side of Will sat his father, Bo, who flipped aimlessly through a Sunday School Booklet.

As the choir sang, the power of their voices vibrated from the rafters and settled in Trey's mind. It seemed that lately, Lisa definitely wielded a lot more power in his life than Jesus—or anyone else for that matter. He wondered if that was somehow sinful.

Before he could arrive at an answer, the choir finished singing and Pastor John Paul stepped to the pulpit, arranged his bible and notes, cleared his throat, and stared out across the congregation. He was a tall man, four inches over six feet, and on a good day, would tip the scales at one hundred and seventy pounds. With deeply sunken eyes of pale blue and a long hawk-like nose, he looked like a taller version of Jim Carey's character in the movie, *A Series of Unfortunate Events*.

"Good morning and God bless." His voice was a deep raspy baritone when he spoke.

The service lasted the customary forty-five minutes. Will and Maggie listened intently, Bo leafed through his Sunday school lesson for the following week, and Trey fiddled with his cellphone. Twenty minutes into the sermon, he received a text message from Lisa.

Where are you? she wanted to know.

Trey quickly texted back, *At church.*

Why didn't you text me this morning when you got up? came the next question.

I thought you might not be awake yet.

Trey noticed that his grandmother was watching him.

I would have gotten it when I woke up, you should have texted. Trey could almost feel Lisa scowling all the way from the Bahamas. Maggie shook her head and patted him on the leg. Trey blushed when he realized his grandmother had seen the texts.

The rest of the service was a blur. Once at a high school baseball practice, he had been standing too close to the batter's box, waiting for his turn to bat, and a foul ball had struck him on the side of the head and knocked him out cold. For days afterwards, he had suffered the effects of a concussion. Most of the time, everything seemed foggy, not unlike the feeling he felt now. He wondered if this was what love was supposed to feel like or if something was wrong with him. Every time Lisa was angry or even just unhappy with him, he felt like he had been dropped in a box and the lid had been slammed shut. It was hard to breathe, and it felt like a huge weight was pressed against his chest.

It had not always been this way. The years they dated in high school had been nice. Of course, there was little for them to disagree on back then and Trey had learned early on it was better if he just went along with her wishes than to deal with her anger. It had not been until she had been invited to join a sorority that things had begun to change. At first, he had been excited for her and even talked about trying to get into a fraternity so they could do things together. When it became clear this was not a part of her plans, they had argued. It seemed like life had been one never ending argument afterwards. He hoped that once she returned from her Bahama trip, she would put all of that behind her and their life would return to the way it had been.

*****

Maggie felt her grandson's tension and put an arm around his shoulders. She slowly and methodically patted his shoulder, and by the end of the sermon, the tension was almost gone. The pastor prayed, then dismissed the congregation.

"Let's go get some lunch," Maggie suggested.

"Y'all might as well ride with us," Will said and headed toward the front door.

*****

120

Trey gave his father a questioning look. Bo just gave him one of his 'you'll figure it out soon' grins and followed along after Maggie and Will. Trey shook his head and fell in behind his father.

At the door, the pastor was shaking hands and wishing everyone a blessed week. Trey stopped long enough to exchange brief pleasantries and had just stepped outside when someone grabbed his arm and squeezed it. He turned and looked straight into the darkest eyes he had ever seen.

"You're Trey Tucker, right?" the young lady asked.

"Yeeees," He stammered feeling the red creep up his neck and the lid on Lisa's box slamming shut. He had an enormous urge to look around to see if Lisa was watching the scene unfold.

"I'm Lupita, Coral's little sister." The girl flashed a bright smile.

"Okay?" Trey could not hide his confusion.

"Coral, Coral Jones, you graduated with her." Lupita raised one dark eyebrow.

"Oh, Coral Jones, yes." Trey finally nodded.

"Sorry to bother you," Lupita apologized, "but I promised Coral I'd tell you Hi the next time I saw you at church. She lives in Phoenix with her husband. He's in the Air Force. Anyway, Hi from Coral."

"Thanks, tell her I said hello back if you would please." Trey said.

"Sure will." She turned and was gone.

Trey turned to look for his father and grandparents and found them grouped in front of a recent model black crew cab Chevy Silverado. He realized all three of them had been watching the exchange between him and Lupita. His grandfather looked pissed, his grandmother looked sad, and his father was grinning like a shit eatin' 'possum. Trey felt completely lost as he moved towards the trio wondering where his grandfather's old white Chevy truck had gone, and why they were all going to lunch together. Nothing seemed to make much sense today.

121

As Trey approached, Will opened the rear door and assisted Maggie into the backseat of the black Silverado. Bo opened the passenger door and climbed in. With a shake of his head, Trey rounded the truck and opened the back-passenger side door as Will pulled the driver's door closed.

"New truck?" Trey queried.

"No, your Pappy just had his old white one painted black," Bo smarted off.

"Bo, you behave yourself," Maggie scolded.

Will chuckled. "Wonder where he gets that shit?"

"You know dang well where he gets it," Maggie said sharply adding, "and it's Sunday, William Henry Tucker, so you watch your language."

"Yes, ma'am." He suppressed another chuckle, but not the grin.

Will backed onto Fourth Street and started south. After two blocks, he turned left past the Fort Cobb United Methodist Church onto Main Street. Two blocks after that, he pulled into a space in front of Pat's Café and Saloon. Named for its owner, Patrick O'Donnell, the building was a massive two-story, red brick building. Trey remembered the first time his grandfather had brought him to eat here. Will had told him that the building had originally been a furniture store. Shortly after it had gone out of business, Pat had shown up with his wife, Sam, short for Samantha, purchased the place, remodeled it, and opened a combination café and saloon.

Trey loved Pat's. He loved the western décor, the mismatched tables and chairs, but most of all the food. Normally, he would have been more than happy with Pappy's choice of diners, but traditionally, the after-church meal was chicken-fried steaks, corn-on-the-cob, mashed potatoes and gravy, and Granny's homemade hot rolls. And usually, it was made and served by Granny at the big house out at the ranch. Confused and wary, he entered the café with his family.

Inside, Will weaved a path through the restaurant to the far back of the room and chose a table for four. He pulled a chair out for Maggie and pushed it forward gently as she seated herself. Then he took the chair beside her with his back to the wall. Bo sat down beside his father and Trey took the remaining chair.

"I've always loved this place," Trey said to no one in particular.

"Ain't gonna find nothin' like this in Tulsa." Will sneered as he unrolled his cloth napkin, removed the utensils, and arranged them on the table in front of himself.

"Now, Will." Maggie placed her hand over his and squeezed.

Trey watched as his grandfather visibly relaxed under her touch. He had seen it many times before, but it always amazed him the way his grandmother could erase anger and frustration with a simple touch.

"What's going on?" Trey asked, "I feel like I've missed something."

"Everything's fine," Maggie told her grandson. "Let's just eat, then we'll talk about a little trip your Pappy and I have planned."

"Will Tucker takin' a trip? Well don't that beat all?" Samantha O'Donnell, Pat's wife and their waitress, interrupted and then asked, "Is everyone having the usual?"

The usual was a grilled chicken breast blanketed with a slice of Monterey Jack cheese and covered with a mixture of sautéed mushrooms, jalapenos, and onions, served with an order of steamed broccoli for Maggie. A nine-ounce Sirloin steak cooked medium rare, a loaded baked potato, and a side salad with ranch for Will. Bo's order matched his fathers and Trey's steak was medium well with a double order of French fries. Everyone wanted the usual.

As Sam headed for the kitchen with their orders, the front doors opened and more of the after-church lunch rush arrived. By the time Trey and his family got their meals, every table in the dining room was taken and several patrons had slipped through the archway that separated the café from the saloon and taken seats at tables there. The smell of food filled both rooms, and the hum of a dozen or more conversations filled the air. Someone laughed across the room. Trey cut a slice from his steak, placed it in his mouth, and felt the flavor of the lightly charred meat dance across his taste buds. It felt so good to be home, even if it was just for the summer.

The buzz of his cell phone indicated he had a text from someone. He pulled it from his pocket and checked to see who had sent it.

Where are you? It was Lisa.

Quickly, he laid his fork aside and texted back, *At Pat's.*

Why? flashed across the screen almost immediately, and even without a voice, the message that Lisa was angry was loud and clear.

Eating with Pappy, Granny, and Dad. He flushed as he hit send.

Why? You usually have lunch at your Granny's came the next message.

"Can't that wait?' Will asked looking at his grandson as he slid a piece of steak into his mouth.

I'll call you later. Trey texted quickly, nodding at his grandfather.

Whatever. Came the reply.

The meal continued without interruption, and soon Sam stopped by to inquire about desserts. Maggie declined, while Will and Bo asked for a slice of pecan pie, and Trey ordered blackberry cobbler with vanilla ice cream on top. Sam gathered as many of the dirty plates as she could carry and returned to the kitchen. Minutes later, she returned with the pie and cobbler.

"Okay, I've waited long enough. What's going on here?" Trey demanded. "And what is this little trip you and Pappy are taking?"

Maggie smiled sweetly. "We're going to California."

"Really?" Trey looked at his grandmother in surprise and took a bite of cobbler and ice cream.

"Yes," She replied, "and *you're* going to drive us."

Trey wasn't sure if he was going to spew the cobbler across the table into his grandfather's lap or choke on it. He tried to swallow. When that didn't work, he tried to chew. California? He could not go to California. What was Granny thinking? What would Lisa say? Oh, she would say plenty. She would use screws to fasten the lid on the box and then bury it six feet deep. This was not part of *her* plan. He tried to swallow again. Still a no go. How could he say no to Granny? She and Pappy had been so good to him. But how could he go to California? This was not good. Not good at all. With difficulty, he managed to swallow.

Laying his spoon down, he finally managed a hoarse whisper, "Seriously?"

"Yes, darling," Maggie confirmed.

Trey looked to his grandfather. Will winked and smiled, "Leavin' in the morning, bright and early."

Bo spoke up before Trey's mind could fashion another question, "You take good care of your Granny and Pappy when y'all are on the road, you hear?"

Without thinking, Trey answered, "Yes, sir."

THE NEON CHURCH JOURNAL

When you've dug the hole so deep you can no longer see the light above, it's time to put the shovel down and start climbing.

Hank has hit rock bottom and storm clouds are gathering on the horizon. Does he have what it will take to turn it all around? Can he become the father his son needs?

He has fifty-two weeks to get it figured out.

ABOUT THE AUTHOR

Charles Lemar Brown is a retired high school science teacher, who now spends much of his time writing and traveling. He is also an avid photographer whose photographs have been sold around the world. He lives in rural Love County, Oklahoma, where he enjoys spending time with his seven children and nineteen grandchildren. Left alone too long, he is likely to be found making TikTok's, working out in his home gym, or kicked back with his cat, Tilee, watching whatever football game he can find on the television. His favorite quote is—what doesn't kill you makes you stronger and I ain't dead yet.